Planetary Brother

Other Books by Bartholomew

"I Come As a Brother": *A Remembrance of Illusions*

From the Heart of a Gentle Brother

Journeys with a Brother: *Japan to India—Bartholomew and the Dalai Lama in the Himalayas*

Reflections of an Elder Brother: *Awakening from the Dream*

All of the above books may be ordered directly from:

White Dove International
P.O. Box 1000
Taos, NM 87571

or by calling Hay House, Inc., at **(800) 654-5126**

ॐ ॐ ॐ

Informal tapes of 600 recorded sessions with Bartholomew, as well as information on talks by Mary-Margaret Moore, may be ordered from:

Mary-Margaret Moore
P.O. Box 1414
Ranchos de Taos, NM 87557

ॐ ॐ ॐ

Please visit the Hay House Website at: **www.hayhouse.com**

Planetary Brother

Bartholomew

HAY HOUSE

Hay House, Inc.
Carlsbad, CA

Published and distributed in the United States by:
Hay House, Inc., P.O. Box 5100, Carlsbad, CA 92018-5100
(800) 654-5126 • (800) 650-5115 (fax)

Edited by: Joy Franklin, Mary-Margaret Moore, and Jill Kramer
Designed by: Wendy Lutge

The author of this book does not dispense medical advice or prescribe the use of any technique as a form of treatment for physical or medical problems without the advice of a physician, either directly or indirectly. The intent of the author is only to offer information of a general nature to help you in your quest for emotional and spiritual well-being. In the event you use any of the information in this book for yourself, which is your constitutional right, the author and the publisher assume no responsibility for your actions.

Library of Congress Cataloging-in-Publication Data

Bartholomew (Spirit)
     Planetary Brother / Bartholomew ; [edited by Joy Franklin,
Mary-Margaret Moore, and Jill Kramer]. — Rev. ed.
        p.   cm.
     ISBN 1-56170-388-5 (trade pbk.)
     1. Spirit writings. 2. Kramer, Jill.   I. Franklin, Joy.
II. Moore, Mary-Margaret.   III. Title.
BF1301.B358   1999
133.9'3—dc21
                                       98-55705
                                          CIP

Originally published by High Mesa Press in 1991.

ISBN: 1-56170-388-5

02 01 00 99 4 3 2 1
First Printing Hay House Edition, April 1999

Printed in the United States of America

This book is gratefully dedicated
to Bartholomew, Buddha,
The Christos, and Ramana Maharshi.

Contents

PART I: CHALLENGE

PART II: JOURNEY

Preface

Six years to the month have gone by since the first Bartholomew book was "typeset" on an Apple computer and published on a "shoestring." Back in those days, 40 or so people would gather at a private home in Albuquerque to share an hour with "him." The equipment we used to record the sessions was hardly the best, and the tapes came out scratchy because none of us realized how precious this teaching would become. Over the years, the equipment improved, the house became an auditorium, and the books were handed over to a professional typesetter. We've upgraded the presentation, but Bartholomew's wisdom has never changed. It still packs the same wallop of truth—the same humor, compassion, and love. The messages may vibrate with greater intensity, but Bartholomew remains a gentle brother.

This fourth book really contains ten keys. Some were hand-forged by people participating in workshops. Others were practiced into reality. Several will fit the lock on your heart. And a few are shaped like bells going off in the empty sky. Find the one that most appeals to you, follow any path to its end, and use the key of your choice to unlock the door to your freedom.

— Editor

Introduction

I wrote the following introduction in the fall of 1990, a few months after we were told that the spoken, public, "outer" work with Bartholomew would come to an end sometime in 1995. Now, in the fall of 1998, I feel the need to reprint it, and to report some "current" insights on the "conclusions" reached in 1990, both mine and others.

It is fall again in my mountain valley, and as I watch the turning of the leaves, I find myself pondering what to say in this, my fourth introduction to a Bartholomew book. So much has been explained and described in those first three introductions that I ask myself what remains. Only one area stands out, and that is to answer the question that has been asked by myself and others many times in the last few months: "How does it feel to know that all of this will be over by the middle of 1995, and what does it mean?"

The answer isn't simple. A part of me is excited when thinking of the time that will be mine to create a new kind of life. The possibilities are glorious, but I am mostly attracted to attempting to put down, through some artistic medium, all the wondrous visual images that have passed through my awareness these past 14 years. Working as the "channel" for this energy has gifted me beyond description. The images are all alive, translucent, reflecting a beauty, luminosity, and depth I have not seen with my ordinary eyes. The excitement and challenge to find out if I am capable of this rendering feels wonderful and scary, all at the same time.

But then, there is "the other side." This other side of me has spent much of my recent life living with this energy in an intimate working relationship—active, public, and global. All of us who work closely with the Bartholomew energy refer fondly to "him" as "The Boss." We use that title in the very best and most respectful way possible. There is absolutely no question that I will greatly miss working with and for "The Boss." So there is a certain sadness about it all, but a soft and gentle sadness, filled with memories of great love, humor, and power.

So what does it all mean? Having pondered this question these past months, I have come to a few "conclusions," which, like all Earthly conclusions, are subject to change. The first conclusion: This is happening because it is the best for all of us concerned, no matter what our fears might tell us. I have trusted the wisdom of this energy for so long and in so many ways that I find it easy to trust in this way as well. If "he" says it's time to end, then it is the end of an absolutely awe-inspiring, exciting, and dynamic experiment, one that I am so very glad to have been a part of. Many people ask if I don't resent in some way my life having been turned upside down for all these years, but the answer is, I have nothing but gratitude for it all.

The second conclusion is: It is happening because we need to be "lights unto ourselves." The thrust of the Bartholomew information has always been, "Find your way. You can do it. What you seek is closer than your breath. It is everywhere. So find it *now* because you are It." We will have the opportunity to do just that. I feel an absolute assurance that we wouldn't be asked to do it "alone" if we didn't have the ability to succeed.

The last conclusion: Bartholomew isn't really going anywhere. It is true that "he" will no longer speak in the familiar form, but "he" has said endlessly, "There is no place to go. It is all right here. If it isn't here, it isn't anywhere." Bartholomew's statements of this nature remind me of the words of Ramana Maharshi. When he was dying, his disciples became afraid. His response sounds like something Bartholomew would say. "Where would I go?" So we have the opportunity to look upon this as an exciting task of finding out the truth of those words. Since in all of my years working with this energy I have found only truth, I have no fear of the outcome.

$$\oint\ \oint\ \oint$$

Bartholomew has stated again and again that there are two basic truths: There is only One, and there are no separations within that One. If there are no separations, then we cannot lose anything, as we and Bartholomew and all the rest of createdness must exist in one glorious Whole.

My first conclusion was that the "leaving" was for the best for all concerned. I have no way of knowing if this proved to be true for those who loved him who are no longer in touch with me, but I can say with absolute truthfulness that for myself and many whom I am still in contact with that it is so.

In the words of one who was very close to him, "Calling on Bartholomew intensifies awareness of that place within us where he has always been." True. When we remember, there IT IS. Of course that energy is always there, but in our outward movement in the world, it can be overlooked. But once looked for, even for an instant, the response is intense and direct. The Comforter is present. Not that our "problems" get solved, but peace and comfort and the feeling of "All's Well" is palpably present. The Presence is Present.

The second conclusion, that we were now meant to be "lights to ourselves," is easily seen when you look at the lives of so many of his "friends." Many of us ARE less outwardly seeking for other teachers or other paths, but are finding that the path is always within, right here, right now. Not that other wise and aware people are not listened to and appreciated, and not that they don't also point to that place where Truth is. But there is no longer the belief that "someone out there" is going to "give it to us." There remains the quiet, subtle knowing that all that is required is to relax into the moment, to be silent, and there IT IS, the ISNESS of God, the Truth of what has always been here.

The third, that Bartholomew wasn't really going anywhere, and has been witnessed over and over again. The letters and calls that I receive have shown me this, beginning in the very first months and continuing until today, almost four years later. For many, the connection is stronger and more readily available, just by the nature of not having to think of it being in any way connected to the body and mind called "Mary-Margaret."

His parting words to us were, "If you miss me, then go to where I have always been, in the very core of your Being. I am that Peace Itself, that Silence Itself. There is only One. How could 'I' ever be separate from the Self, which is also 'your' Self? Inquire within, without thinking and conceptualizing, and you will experience that there is no separation, anywhere."

No day passes without my (and many others) feeling the deepest gratitude for this mysterious "Happening-in-Consciousness" playfully named "Bartholomew" that led us ever deeper into what was always here, our True Nature, which is the Light of Awareness Itself. Are we aware of anything? Then Awareness, which is another name for God, for the Self, is also present, here, now. And that, as I now understand, is what Bartholomew was all about.

—Mary-Margaret Moore

PART I

Challenge

to have them be. You must first make a decision. Either you let your mind dwell in fear over ways to survive all the horrors that are possible, or keep remembering that *excitement* is what you are feeling inside. Whatever the fear in the mind, the soul is capable of feeling not trepidation, but excitement! Please take a few moments to let that concept sink into your mind.

Take a deeper look at your world. Perhaps it is time for some things in it to change. Humanity as a whole is very definitely divided into those who have and those who do not have. Your inner being knows that it would feel best for this planet to have equality, to have a sense of wonder and unity filling everyone on it. This awareness is part of each one of you. So instead of interpreting change as fearful, ask yourself if the feeling could be described as something else. Could there be a sense of excitement in the potential of the next coming years? Could this new way of feeling help you in a maximum push for freedom from fear? That is what we need to discuss.

§ § §

Let us talk a bit about all these psychic predictions that keep filling people's hearts and minds. Do you remember the story about a woman who predicted that the great San Francisco earthquake was going to happen on April 19th? Since she lived in San Francisco, she was afraid of this event and had spent much time worrying about it. One night she had a dream. In the dream, she saw the bridges of San Francisco falling, and people dying, and saw the date, April 19, filling the sky. She felt she had seen a future event. Others who believed her changed their lifestyles completely in order to be in a place they thought would be safe. But the woman had misinterpreted the dream—*she* died on April 19th, and San Francisco remained unchanged.

What is the point? There are many things in the world today that can fill you with fear. For instance, when it comes to believing what psychic channels have said, it is your *obligation* to determine their validity, not by what they say, but by what your heart and mind tell you. Do you *feel* it to be truth? Do you feel you have the *ability* to know such things? I am asking that you stop listening to disaster channels and attune your listening to a vaster frequency. Listen to energies that resonate within you with hope, understanding, and expansion. There is magic in this wonderful Earth experiment that you are undergoing, and the greatest magic will be the manifestation of a great frequency of God-Consciousness on this planet. And it *is* worth doing. If you wallow in future fears and ignore present power, your life will begin to reflect fear, and soon that is all you will see. Choose to dwell on beauty, love, and hope, and this will fill your life. Remember the basic teaching—what *you* dwell upon becomes real *for you.*

As a part of a wonderful unfoldment of consciousness, you have the potential to come into the full knowing of yourself as a part of that God-Awareness in the next decade. To maximize the coming opportunities, you *must* understand that feeling fear or feeling the excitement of awakening lies not in what happens physically on the planet, but rather, what happens in your mind.

It is your *mind* that creates your heaven and your hell, using whatever outer circumstances surround you. You cannot decide what this planet will do, whether governments will rise or fall, or whether as a species you will survive. As an individual mind and body, you have very little knowledge of what would be maximum for the wholeness of the planet. But there is one thing you do know. Your individual life, which impinges on those around you, either expands and gives the gifts of peace, humor, love, compassion, and courage; or it does the opposite. That *is* under your control; and it is you, moment after moment, thought after thought, action after action, who decides which world you will create. You have tremendous opportunities to infuse your life with the gifts of consciousness, so don't let those opportunities slip past as you gaze upon your future.

You know, my friends, in this world of yours there is a lot of discussion about devils and angels. The devil does all the bad things, and the angels do all the good things, in an everlasting battle of good against evil. As an allegory, it's fascinating, but as a reality, what does it have to do with you? Everything! The same dynamic is going on in your mind and the minds of others on the planet. You are in a mental battle between good and evil. With every thought you think, every action you perform, and every wish you have, you are making a choice as to which side of these vast energy fields you are going to support. And the one you support the most has the greatest influence on your life.

It is a mistake to think that your finite mental process has nothing to do with what the energy fields you call God and the devil are and will become. Your ego delivers a very lethal message. It says, "Go ahead and have all the negative thoughts you want, because there's always next month or next year or the next incarnation to change them." And, my friends, there may be, but do any of you *really* know that there is such a thing as reincarnation? Really? You read about it, talk about it, and have what you call past-life recollections, but have you *experienced* reincarnation? If you do not know that "other lifetimes" are real, why wait? Why not make maximum effort *now*? Some Earthly times are more useful for Enlightenment than others; and these next years, my friends, are the times when the opportunity is maximum. Don't sleep it away. Awaken.

You don't need to completely believe all we have said, but believe it just enough to be serious about doing all those things you have so long postponed, just serious enough to begin all the loving thoughts and loving acts you have not quite gotten around to having and doing. The next ten years will give you a marvelous opportunity to answer the question of consciousness, which is: *Who are you?* You do not know! This is why you cannot state with absolute surety that "I know I am a reincarnative being." What if this is your only life? I am not trying to frighten you. I am trying to awaken you to the awareness of that soft, unceasing voice of the ego that will continue to tell you what you feel, do, or say today doesn't matter, because you can always change it tomorrow.

৶ ৶ ৶

The number of distractions is infinite these days. You no longer need two people to be really distracted from what is going on in your life. With the universal mandala of the television, one person can be totally distracted by nonpeople's nonproblems. You live longer, so there are more of you here, and more of you playing the game of life. The game keeps getting bigger and more complex, and the rules are constantly changing. There is always the question of whom to love and whom to hate, whom to embrace and whom to turn away from. All of these questions are acted out on a planetary scale as well as within your own country, your own city, your own home, and your own self. The ego is to be congratulated for its ability to provide such a great diversification of distractions! They are endless and will continue in ever-increasing volume and frequency, unless you begin to mute the voices.

There is often no one in control of your thoughts—certainly not you! The repetitive patterns of your past have been set through trial and error, and the past grinds out your thoughts day after day. This repetition gives you a sense of continuity, because you are still thinking many of the same thoughts today you were thinking ten years ago. Thus, you can support the belief that there is a consistent "you." The ego wants you to feel continuity because it wants you to think continuity brings you safety. It further says that the only happiness the "you" that you think you are will ever have, is when you are ***right***—when you feel yourself to be "better than" others. I suggest you take that basic premise apart by questioning if being right, being "better," has brought you happiness in the past.

Is it really true that all you need is an accumulation of "right" to make you happy? If you are right more than wrong during your life, will you then die happy? Do you need to be more right than wrong, or more right than anyone else to be an Enlightened One? Let's ask Jesus about that. Jesus was Enlightened, and at the end, the world did not see him as "right." In fact, they saw him as so wrong they killed him.

The ego doesn't want you to look too closely at such questions, so *you* must bring them into consciousness for close examination. The ego would much prefer that you continue the soft, gentle, rocking motion between good and evil, right and wrong, me and you, us and them. It is this movement that keeps you asleep, and I am trying to cut the strings of the hammock. There must be something going on here that doesn't have anything to do with this kind of hierarchy, something more than just the cry of "Let me be right!"

What is it, and how do you find it? Begin by uncovering and examining those areas in which you are absolutely addicted to being right, whom you are addicted to being right over, and which of your righteous beliefs you are willing to defend. Is it the way you cut your green beans? Do you cut them French style, or do you cut them straight? You are laughing, but watch yourself at Christmas dinner. As you are adding butter to the mashed potatoes, and somebody else wants you to use margarine, watch your feelings. Observing your small responses can lead to great understanding, so *watch* them.

Most of you consider being nonjudgmental as something you do when big events are afoot. So you watch for these and usually do very well. You can be "forgiving" over large issues, but you are not as likely to be forgiving over how your mate drives the car, where they put their socks, or whether they leave the toilet seat up or down. I am very serious. I am bringing this to the most mundane level because that is where the ego hypnotizes you, saying such judgments are too small to matter. You allow them to go on because "they are not so important," and besides, "everyone has them." On the other hand, when you find out that your lover is having an affair, you say, "This is serious. This is so serious that I want to be open, receptive, clear, and do my best to understand it."

All the best comes forward in the worst of times, and those victories are wonderful, but the important moment comes with, who let the dog out? It's two in the morning and the dog is out, so who's going to let the dog in? Well, who let it out? Your relationship comes to a particular point over which you keep grinding out the same message—who is going to be right? The person who doesn't have to get up and let the dog in sees himself as right. Interestingly enough, the person who gets up to let the dog in sees herself as right also because she "gave in." She stomped to the door and yanked it open and slammed it shut, but is "right" because she is the one who "really cares." It's the little things that get you, my friends. I am trying to impress this on you so you will wake up to your condition and be serious about making other choices in the coming years.

There is no turning back when you are truly ready to experience who you are. You are on your way, and nothing can stop that kind of willingness, that kind of devotion to your own knowing and your own power. You can start to experience who you are by using a technique that may sound trite and simple, but is not easy. Begin by viewing your mind as a motor, constantly running on and on about an endless number of things. Acknowledge this, and then simply watch it working. Just as you can calm unruly children simply by quietly watching them, this kind of soft observation is very helpful to the quieting down of your mind.

Have you ever tried looking at one thought steadily? Try it. It is very difficult, and the strain you experience doing it will show you how hard it is. So be gentle. Instead of grasping at each individual thought, just try to get the general drift of thinking. Become aware that there is an energy field we will call *you* watching the rise and fall of something called *thought.* As you do this, you will get closer to that part of you that is awakening to its fullness. It is your True Self that is watching the rise and fall of thoughts and the rise and fall of emotions.

For example, you are sitting in a room and the door slams. A feeling of irritation comes over you. You describe your response by saying that something has triggered emotion and you feel irritated. If you slow the process down, you will find that it begins with a thought. The thought is triggered by the sound of a banging door and is not usually a very serious matter, but you find yourself irritated. Then you spend 10 or 15 minutes being irritable. If someone else happens to walk in during that time, it is quite possible that your response will be, "Why did you slam the door?" Now you have pulled someone else into it, *it* being the reaction pattern of ego-consciousness. If you want to stop that reaction pattern, you have to start practicing the gentle, detached observation of the rise and fall of your thoughts and emotions.

Just because you have an emotion such as irritation does not mean you have to act on it. You do not have to constantly remind a person who has hurt you of what they have done. You do not have to smile with sweet patience. You do not have to respond at all. To *not* respond would be to break a pattern, and breaking those habitual responses is useful. Then you find you have other choices. At that moment, understanding you are experiencing a feeling brought about by a thought, you can choose to let it go. You can choose not to have a 20-minute dialogue either inner or outer, on the slamming door. You can choose to move attention away from the thoughts and the emotions, and drift down through it all to rest in that inner place where peace, silence, and non-judgmental power are. That is the choice you can always make.

I am suggesting a ten-year program of self-observation. Every time you track down any of your repetitive responses, you will add to your understanding of how ego patterns work. Whenever you feel one of those small patterns pushing against the surface of your consciousness, whether it's self-pity, anger, jealousy, or any of the others, it is time to get serious. It is an opportunity. It is, if you will, God's way of getting your attention, letting you know that under the surface of these simplistic little responses lies something very big and important. You don't have to mine the entire mountain of responses to get at the gold that is buried in each particle of that mountain. Every time those feelings come up, you can examine them; and the instant the examination is over, you can drop them and go back to that still, inner place.

This is where healing happens. Any time you choose to move out of the repetitive pattern of painful thoughts, no matter how real they feel, you will find that by just allowing yourself to fully concentrate on and feel these thoughts, they leave. When you are willing to face and experience them fully, they leave. This is healing. Healing happens a hundred thousand times a thousand ways, and you really don't know how. There is no denying that life can be painful. You are ready to be healed when you are ready to ask for it, which means that enough rage or self-pity has been released so that what remains is a deep desire to end the pain and separation. All healing comes from God, so that power is always in you; and when you call upon it with sincerity, it can rise and fill in the cracks of a psyche that has been hurt and separated by real damage. You call such things miracles. You can have these miracles a hundred times a day by asking and waiting expectantly, knowing it can happen.

As you move through these next dynamic years with power, you will begin to feel something new growing inside you. It is not just a feeling of anticipation, but something slightly unfamiliar. Please do your best not to decide what it is, because once you define it, you will dismiss it. Keep your awareness open, and allow this very real feeling to arise. Because you have words to describe something like God, the ego feels that it has done its job. It rationalizes that, since you understand God to be omniscient and omnipresent, no more is needed. This same rationalization arises when you start to study your thoughts. *You really believe you understand your thoughts because you think them.* But thoughts move through you like wind through the trees. You don't come to understand them by paying attention to the movement of every thought, but by getting a "felt sense" of *thinking*.

Thinking is an immense energy field that moves through your physical body. Just as air moves in wind, so does thought move in your mind. Thinking implies motion. A thought moves into your mind, then it moves out. When you choose to step back from fixating on each thought and watch the whole process instead, you create distance. You move from short-sighted to far-seeing.

The choice is yours, my friends. Where are you going to go to find peace? A part of you is pretending to be unconscious, but *you are not!* The totality of you knows that something wonderful is afoot. Your picture of the planet as alive and full of light is, for the first time in the history of this planet, global in scope. And it's people like you, all over the world, who are going to make this global union happen. But you must decide whether it is the excitement, wonder, and hope for this planet that will rest in your heart, or the fragmented belief in all the possible separations.

As the planet moves toward Wholeness, every one of you has the same opportunity. It is a magic time, and you were wise to pick this time to be here. Between now and when next we meet, many things will have happened on this planet and in your own life. Don't be fooled. The small feelings will tell you that something needs to be looked at. It's that small surge of superiority, of righteousness, of judgment, of anger that needs your attention.

The big things will fall into place. This discrimination is vital. Please remember, every moment of your life is holy. Be alive. Pay attention. No more sleeping. You deserve the honor of your own awareness, so live your life fully and experience it.

2

The Curtain of Separation

Many of you have been coming to these monthly meetings for years and have commented that things have changed for you due to these hours spent together. But what is it that happens exactly? Does "just sitting here" make a difference?

§ § §

The answer is simple. You really begin to learn, transform, or change anything when you are *engaged* on your side of a process. Coming to sharings like these makes it easy to just sit and listen, and while listening, to pretend something is changing in you. Your ego-mind tries to convince your Deep Self that you've done your part by just being here. Therefore, you say it is up to Bartholomew to change things. But what is happening from "my" side of this is quite different. "I" am waiting to sense a spiritual yearning or a slight expansion in your awareness. The moment is present in even the smallest increment, and I have the ability and desire to move instantly into that space and open up your awareness to stretch your experience of your connection to the Divine. But until you present that opportunity, my friends, *I can do nothing.*

I sometimes use the term *windbag* to describe this process called Bartholomew in order to show you the similarity between your experience of "me" and your experience of the wind. When you are outdoors with the wind blowing around you, you become very aware of your relationship to it. You feel its presence just as you feel my energy. If you choose to go into your house, you will still hear the wind or the sound of my voice, but you will no longer be participating fully with the experience of being together. So there is a difference between these two positions. If you are inside, only listening to the sound of wind, that experience does not make you intimate with the role wind plays in transforming and moving things around. What does is your part in this process. You must be open and aware—alive to what is. Listen. See. Breathe. Be fully there.

I am asking you to quietly and powerfully prepare these openings in yourself. This can be done through the willingness to experience whatever is present. The experience then becomes real; and it can move into you, permeate you, and make you more porous. When you become more porous, you allow the Light that is seemingly outside to enter and join with the Light that is seemingly inside of you. That joining illuminates the wonderful, combustible state we call Enlightenment. You become the radiant *experience* of the Light and not just the intellectual mentalization of it. So, if we can, I would like to spend this year thinning the veil between what you consider to be "outside" and "inside" of you.

The Light that you call God is a vast, magnificently alive, totally loving, totally compassionate energy source present everywhere. And inside you is exactly the same thing. There is no difference between what you call outer space, or emptiness, and the space that is present within you. What keeps you from experiencing this unified energy field as *one thing* is the thickness of the veil between them. *There is no difference between the Light within and the Light without.* But there appears to be a veil, keeping this knowledge out of your reach.

Now, remember the basics. Your physical, mental, and emotional bodies "chatter" a great deal. Since they are always in motion, they create a lot of noise or static that you continually pay attention to. You ignore the sound of the space within and the space without. So the job is simply to decrease the static that creates what seems to be this very thin veil between these power sources. When they *do* join in your awareness, the veil disappears and you see the unreality of the static producing ego-self. Although some identity remains and you know there is still a body that has to do all of its bodily things, you also know it to be an impermanent, very gossamer vessel that can at any time be removed as the center of your focus. You can then focus your awareness on the One Self, and not on the separated parts. You become aware of the Self. You know Who You Are.

What is necessary to do this is your *willingness* to have the outer and inner space join so the static is no longer experienced. You create pain in yourselves when you butt up against these two energy fields. Pain is *not* a part of the inner Light, and pain is *not* a part of the outer Light. It arises from the motion of the veil you have created between them. These two parts of the same power are always flowing, trying to come together, constantly yearning to blend with one another. *A seeker's goal in life is to experience the coming together of these powers,* because you know it is absolutely essential for your peace and fulfillment.

Haven't you ever wondered what it is that keeps you on the so-called spiritual path? It is this constant pulsating, pulling, and tugging of the Light to join with Itself. You may think it is your intellectual concepts, but in moments of stress, the intellect does not help. In those moments of anger or fear, the mind knows you should be saying, "Peace and love are the answer." So you may say, "Peace and love are the answer," but nothing changes. Concepts are concepts, and they do not have a *sustaining* force to them. What keeps you going in spite of this, what really holds you to the path, is the constant, ongoing desire of these two seemingly separate forces to explosively unite. This desire is a feeling, a yearning—*not* a concept.

The separation arises when you focus all your attention on that gossamer veil hung between these two energy fields, It's as if you have two powerfully dynamic fields trying to come together, with one very thin curtain between them, and everyone is staring at the curtain! All of this incredible energy is present, and you are saying, "Look at this interesting curtain! Look at this painful curtain!" Divine Power is assaulting you from without, and your own inner God is shouting to be heard, but you are transfixed by this curtain. "Look, it's moving over there!" You know what that means. Your problem is your relationship. "Look, now it's blowing over here!" And you know what *that* means. No, it's not the relationship, it's your job. On and on, to and fro, movement after movement.

You keep trying to make sense out of the motions of this thin, undulating curtain. It's blown now here, now there, so you want something to explain it. "Ah, if it moves two degrees to the right, it means this!" Then you make great laws about it. You have the laws of philosophy, laws of psychology, laws of religion, endless laws based on the moving curtain moving two degrees to the right. It is these laws that give you a sense of ongoing continuity. You feel safer and more secure if you think you can understand the laws that govern the movements of the curtain. But you cannot make laws about something that is not real.

I would like to tell you something, even though you have heard it before. *You are looking at the wrong thing!* You feel there will be a moment when that curtain, with its infinite number of ripples and tucks, is going to be in perfect alignment; and then you will have the perfect curtain, the perfect life! This drive for curtain perfection is so strong that you spend all your time trying to achieve it. It is humorous, but it is also very painful. No matter how much you try to understand the curtain, you cannot fit it into Divine Law. It follows the law of its own motion, which you know as the motion of *ego*. When you fix your eyes on the motion of the curtain and try to make *cosmic sense* out of it, you are doomed to failure. The motion of the ego curtain is caused by ego energy. So stop looking at the wrong thing.

§ § §

I am going to ask you to quickly complete a sentence for me in your mind. "I am unhappy because . . ."

However you finished that sentence, my friends, has something to do with the motion of the ego curtain. As long as you believe you are unhappy because the curtain is not in a particular place, as long as you believe you will never be happy until the curtain has a particular look, you are doomed to misery, because it changes endlessly. As soon as you have reconciled or resolved one of the folds of the curtain to your liking, look down three inches, and you will find that something else has moved out of place.

Your ego tries to convince you that by paying enough attention to the curtain, you will get it to hang right. How many more lifetimes are you going to believe this? *The motion of the ego curtain has nothing to do with your happiness.* You truly believe when you have a very difficult situation in your life that you would feel more peaceful if this situation were not there. But as painful as your lives are, you need to keep the following in mind: *The coming together of the seemingly separated powers is the only solution to your problems.* Anything else is simply patching the curtain. You can choose one thing over another. You can leave this or you can keep that. You can make endless choices about the curtain, but in the end, it remains a curtain. The problem is not the shape, size, or number of folds it has; *the problem is your transfixed gaze upon it.*

So, remembering your completed sentence: "I am unhappy because . . . ," please acknowledge you are having a problem with your curtain and that it might be very painful. Do not pretend it isn't. Since you exist, you are here, the curtain is here, and the pain is here. Do not deny it. If you think that this time you are going to figure it out, this time it's going to be different—that's looking at the curtain! If you know what your problem looked like yesterday, but you had new thoughts about it last night, you will try and convince yourself that today will bring the perfect curtain. But will it?

It's like coming down with the flu. Ego situations don't come on all at once. You will have a few symptoms before it hits full blast. If you listen to your mind, you can hear the thoughts that are going to bring on your latest bout of curtain flu. This is the point where you can make a different choice. It's as if a greater part of you takes you by the neck and gives you a loving shake. "Stop it! Stop it! How many times are we going to do this?" It is a gentle reminder to be aware of the thoughts, be fully aware of them, and then, please give the Light a chance. Consciously remember those things that make you feel warm and alive inside. They give you a feeling of hope. For some of you it may be remembering that there is an inner and outer Light and your wish to join them together. For others, it may be a remembrance of "I am Peace Itself," or "I am Light, or "I am That."

It is difficult to make this shift by yourself because you think you *are* the curtain. You forget you are so much more than that. The curtain alone does not have the power to cause this magnificent, wonderful explosion to happen. The curtain is of the ego, and it will not choose to destroy itself by allowing this joining to take place. So give yourself a gentle, yet intense, reminder that inside of you is the very same Divine Energy that is outside of you. Remember, you have all the power of the Light at your disposal, should you ask. When you do, it's as if the Love in you breaks out of the heart; and when the heart is open, the Light is released.

Please dwell deeply on this. In religious terms, it is called union with God. Keep the idea in your awareness that there is a Light "within" and a Light "without," and you want to experience the combustion that comes when they join. Pay close attention to the way you feel when you are not engaged with your ego problems. You may be reluctant to let them go. You may find it difficult to stop worrying about them. The ego might tell you that worrying eventually brings understanding, and understanding means peace. But peace does not come from worry. It comes from peace. The ego problems go on endlessly. From the time you wake up in the morning—"Who's going to make the coffee today?"—to the time you go to bed—"Who's going to put the cat out tonight?" In those moments, the way to having this work for you is to experience how it feels to take your attention off the curtain. This requires focusing your attention on letting it go.

Everyone wants pleasure. Whether or not you consciously think about yourself like this, you are still a person who wants pleasure. *How* you define it differs, but the psyche moves toward pleasure, and you must understand that *God is a pleasure.* I have never known anyone to meet the Divine and say, "What a humbug. This God-Enlightening business is boring. I wish I had never tried it. Give me my problems back." This is because God is the *ultimate* pleasure! That being a truth, you are going to move toward *anything* you see as bringing you pleasure. But pay attention to see if you are really in a state of pleasure when you are doing something you *think* will give it to you. You may not be getting as much pleasure from your pleasure as you think you are!

Many people develop addictions because of this. No one becomes addicted because it's painful. They do it because a part of them believes pleasure lies in whatever the addiction is, even if it only offers an opportunity to escape feeling pain. Those people need to pay close attention to what is really happening inside them. When a person deeply experiences that which they thought was going to give pleasure as giving instead a feeling of desperate loneliness and a negative sense of themselves, they will begin to release their hold on the addiction and move to where pleasure really lies.

As we said in the beginning of our sharing, the God Energy is always waiting for the slightest opening to enter. The opening comes when you choose to remove your awareness from those things that are difficult and frightening, and place that awareness on what you know to be your real pleasure. I am asking you to move your thoughts away from one set of beliefs and *trust* that there is a Divine Energy waiting to flood you from within. Put your focus on *real* pleasure, what it is that gives you deep peace and delight, and then choose to move toward it.

Move away from your endless fascination with the ego curtain and you will find that God is there. He is lurking, waiting to grab your heart and hold you. It's very simple, but it's not easy. It must be done moment by moment, thought by thought, action by action. It's not the five-year plan; it's the five-second plan. There are millions of openings to your heart, and they are made as you move away from the curtain and choose to think of the Light. Every time you sit in meditation, you automatically take your awareness off the curtain. When you sit with the intention of becoming still or finding the Light within or feeling the Oneness, that's enough.

You don't need to have everything in perfect order for God to enter. With the slightest movement on your part, the response will be there. *You must test that statement!* I suggest some kind of centering meditation with the intention of having these two Divine energy fields come together. In time, the curtain between them will become very thin, very fragile and illusory; and the awareness of that inner and outer power will become the reality of your life. Do it now or do it later. *You will do it.* You must, because these two energy fields are absolutely addicted to coming together. There is a compulsion from the Heart of God to unite with the God within you; and what God wants, God gets!

I would like to relate a true event that fits in very well with what we are talking about. Dr. Serge King, a teacher of Huna from Hawaii, tells this story. When the Soviet Union was picking their team to go to the 1984 Olympics, they divided the participants into four groups. They were all told that one of these groups would go to the Olympics. The first group trained in the normal fashion. The second group took a fourth of that normal training time and spent it in visualization. They talked with each other and with their advisors about how to train perfectly, and watched television presentations of perfect motion. The third group spent half of their time in this new way, and the last group spent three-fourths of their time visualizing and only one-fourth of their time actively engaged in the physical training.

Obviously, the story ends with the fourth group going to the Olympics, and, as I recall, the Soviet Union did very well. The point here is to understand the principle that motivated their victory, because it's the same principle that will motivate your victory. *It isn't what you do physically that determines the outcome of what you are doing. Outcomes are determined by the belief in the outcome.* Visualization helps determine belief. Look at what you are now visualizing about yourself, about other people in your life, and about difficult situations, and you will find that most of the time you are dwelling on *what is wrong.* There is the curtain again! The story about the Soviet Olympic team dramatically reminds you that the power in this kind of visualization does not come from gazing at the problem. It comes from gazing with complete confidence on what you see as the perfect solution to the situation.

Look at it as a beautiful, delightful dance of awakening. You may not believe it works, but try it anyway! What have you got to lose? That which you concentrate on will come into focus. So ask yourself what pictures you are now showing your psyche. Your psyche will reproduce those pictures for you in your life. This is how you can shift old patterns. It takes mental energy, so go for something vast, something really important, really magnificent, and not something mundane. To ride the crest of your own thought-forms is very difficult in the beginning. Your mind will go off in all directions, while doubts and boredom will arise to block you. You must have the determination that a really vast desire can give you, and you must have the will and patience to see it through. Make the picture of your dream as beautiful, dynamic, and extending as you can; and support it with all the power that you have, and that is what the psyche will reproduce for you.

So what have we said today? If you want Enlightenment, and if you want to feel your heart overflowing with Love, you must remove your awareness from the movement of the ego curtain and place it on those things that will give you the pleasure of connecting with the Divine. If there is some dis-ease in your life that you really feel needs healing or changing, spend the time and energy it takes visualizing what it is you truly want to feel and be. Remember how we began. This God that loves you absolutely and totally is lurking in Its magnificence to move in and join with you, and in that joining, to explode the illusion that you are a lonely, wandering, lost child. It's all there waiting for you. So, good luck, my friends. You can do it. Of that, there is absolutely no doubt.

This God that
loves you
absolutely is
lurking in Its
magnificence
to move in and
join with you.

3

Experience and Consciousness

Day One
Whatever it is, it's God.

*My friends, good morning. I am pleased that we are togeth-
er again to share in this process that is not a process. It is
going to be a journey to a place where you've already arrived, a
search for what you already see, a becoming which you already
are, a longing to be aware when you are already total awareness.
These words describe a mental picture you have of what you
think you are going to find at journey's end. But there is nothing
to find. Nothing is wrong with anything. All is exactly as it is,
which is as it should be. There is nowhere to go, nothing to do,
but we are going to pretend to go and do for the next few days.
Hopefully, as we continue to crack against your belief structures,
they will break open, and you will see, with great amusement, the
hysterical situation your mind has placed you in.*

Let me repeat, the hysterical situation your *mind* has placed
you in. Please get a sense of the two of you. Your mind has created this situation that you find yourself in. Doesn't it seem that
your mind moves along with ease, consciously making decisions
that convince you that your thinking is the creator of your expe-

rience? It isn't that way; it just *seems* that way. If you are willing to wrestle with any paradox long enough, it will become so shaky that old, outmoded belief structures will begin to crumble. So let us present some paradoxes for you to wrestle with.

I want to get you to push against your belief that you know what is really going on in your life. I want you to feel that something is happening here that your brain will simply never understand, and it is *not* necessary for it to understand. You think some awakening is going to happen to you here this week. Something is not *going* to happen. It is happening now! Your ideas that you can pray harder, purify yourself more, and become more holy are false. You are already purified, holy, and filled with prayer!

You see, it's the mind that takes the basic magnificent, pure substance of your Being and twists it into different shapes, some of which are uncomfortable. You wake up in the morning and say things like, "Today I am going to try to be more loving to my husband (or wife). I am going to try to live more with an open heart and see things more clearly. I am going to try to fill myself with peace, love, joy, and beauty." All the while your ego is laughing because all this "trying" is precisely what the ego wants you to do. It wants you to keep looking at these twisted shapes, trying to find out how to untwist them. You try this and try that until you become very trying—to yourselves and each other.

So many of your days end with a feeling of "I didn't make it. The day was wonderful until those last five minutes. My heart was open, I felt peace. I was all those things I wanted to be this morning until I tripped over those shoes someone left in my path and broke my glasses. I became furious and *that* is what I am left with." At those times, do you remember a day of wonder-filled moments, or the last event? And when thinking of the broken glasses, do you feel a constriction of heart and a surge of anger at the circumstance and the other person who caused it all to happen? Then, do you find that you're scolding yourself because you have all these feelings?

This week is an opportunity to come to the realization that any feeling you have, any thought you think, or any action you take *is it.* What we mean by "is it" is *God!* One part of you is searching for a new experience, while another part of you is already experiencing it. *When you get in touch with the part of your Being that is just experiencing, you will begin to find delight in everything!* And when you believe this, you will feel, even immersed in the most deadening fear or raging anger, that there is a part of you experiencing it with *delight.* Bad choice of words? Not at all. The deepest part of you *makes no differentiation* between experiencing good or bad, pleasure or pain. It is just aware of experiencing!

You have been trained to *name* your experiences, and in so doing, spend your lives *thinking* about them. "That feeling is jealousy, and jealousy is bad." *Your ego wants you to think about experience rather than feel it.* The ego loves to have you define your problems. "My problem is, I am not loving." The minute you define it, the ego can either dismiss it because you have defined it, or engage you in an endless round of mental analysis of the problem. Either way, you miss it, because you are no longer feeling. And feeling life every moment is what God is all about. You must become aware of the place where you can feel the *ongoing* experience of life. When you taste that, no matter how short the moment of tasting might be, you begin to *know* what a dynamic, creative force life is.

This is the experience we are after together, and the first step to reaching it is to understand how your mind distracts you. It plays a lot of games that all seem to be very different. You will find that they are not. These form deep patterns of beliefs that make you miserable. They get your attention and create tension in your life. They gather together and form *clusters*, so you become addicted to thinking and acting in different ways about them instead of relaxing into your experience of the event. These thoughts do not have a goal or a destination. They rise and fall constantly, but *do not connect you with anything or anyone.* They are the kinds of thoughts that *separate.*

You all had scenarios in your life where you have "tripped over someone else's shoes and become agitated." When this happens to you, right then is when you can ask, "What is really going on here? What am I feeling inside? Why did I get so angry about that event?" All of the hidden, separating concepts, beliefs, and seeming realities between you and whoever was unfortunate enough "to leave the shoes out," arise instantaneously. These thoughts and feelings lead to other larger areas, usually from the past, and to people and events that have no seeming connection to you and the shoes. Pay attention and follow your thinking and feeling to these larger clusters. Begin to identify them. You will be surprised at what you discover in addition to that first flash of anger. Many past feelings and beliefs "cluster" around what you think might be "just getting angry." As you stay with this process, something mysterious will happen. Things begin to calm down. As the thoughts become conscious and are felt fully, they leave a space.

Do not worry about which thoughts are positive and which are negative. What is a positive thought? A negative thought? The minute we say positive versus negative, we are lost in speculation. You are only thinking about positive and negative. What you need is the experience of what positive and/or negative events *feel* like. To do that, you must become aware of and allow yourself to be the *experiencer.* This means you experience everything—*everything!* The judgmental mind has no role in experiencing.

§ § §

Thoughts are like static, and it's the constantly pulsating static that keeps sending out waves of interference. As you begin to settle down and calm your mind, you'll find this static resurfacing to ensnare you. Anything that wanders past the mind can get your attention. Let's say you are doing something pleasurable and find yourself becoming depressed. *Don't assume you know why.* Don't assume you *know* anything. Gather the facts. Become the detective in the case. Begin an investigation. Investigators do not defend *any* point of view. They simply observe. Observe what is going on inside you with as much openness as you can. Carry a notebook small enough to fit in your purse or pocket, and at the first opportunity, write down all the separating ideas or judgments around whatever has caught your attention. As you do this, you begin to call the game on yourself. This little experiment will be amazingly helpful. The incredible, experiential life is all inside you and it's all "out there" as well. It is possible to remove the separating clusters that keep you from it.

For those of you really ready to experience this, I have a short mantra that you can run through your mind day and night: *Whatever it is, it's God.* You are so used to saying the good, the true, and the beautiful are God; but not the bad, the evil or the ugly. Those differences and judgments are what we have to smooth out. Take your mind off whatever event your ego is trying to convince you is really important, and start putting it on the Divine in that event. *Whatever it is, it's God.* You find yourself totally impatient and angry at some obstacle in front of you. *Whatever it is, it's God.* You've lost your house, your job, your car, and your spouse. Just say it: *"Whatever it is, it's God,"* and then go on to something else.

Identifying the thoughts and feelings that cluster around a particular event will reveal the motion of your mind. Just like a recalcitrant child, it will start to calm down as you observe it without judgment. When an uncomfortable feeling arises, look at it as the benevolent watcher. Listen to it. Write in your notebook the words that describe it. Open it up, and in the opening up, it will begin to move out. The really painful clusters are not only formed by what is in front of you, but by endless beliefs and past events, real or imagined. There is a lot going on in the mind. Look at it quietly and gently. Look at the feelings again and again, and they will reveal their secrets.

§ § §

Tonight, as you practice identifying your clusters, be totally aware of your body. You will miss this experience if you're not in there. When you sit down, don't sit in your brain. Sometimes you don't even know if you are in pain because you are thinking so hard. Today, I am particularly asking you to feel your body, that you have a bottom and it sits on a chair, and feet that are on the floor. You move, you breathe. It's very important. The body is where you connect with an event; where it's going to happen, and where it's already happened. You get closer to yourself by bringing your awareness back inside the body.

This is the process that is not a process. The minute we start to talk, it is gone. But for now, this model is the best we have. So those are the two assignments for today. Watch your mind, identify and record the clusters of thought, and be aware of where it is all taking place.

§ § §

Day Two
Shifting States of Awareness

You are filled with the Divine and present in It, no matter what you are experiencing. Since you are constantly experiencing something, the question is, would you like that experience to be joy-filled with bliss and happiness, or pain-filled with separation and suffering? That's the only question, because God is totally present and alive in both states. You are not farther from God in one state and closer to God in the other. All we are try-

ing to do here together is take the thrust of your awareness, which has been toward pain for many lifetimes, and simply and gently detach it so you can choose to let it rest elsewhere.

Just pull the plug and relax. I asked you to spend last evening with an exercise that would keep you aware of what is happening in your mind. This was the beginning of the disconnection. You always have the option to disconnect yourself from the ego distractions of the world. Every moment *you* decide where your awareness is going to go. Let me give you a few examples of your choices. You can put your awareness on what it feels like to be totally present in the physical, or take your awareness and move it out into the manifest world, interacting with each other and feeling the world around you. A third choice is to take your awareness into the realm of the mental where fantasy lies, where you rerun the past, and where you project into the future.

§ § §

Right now, I would like us to practice placing awareness in each of these three areas. What you will gain is the delight of knowing you can choose to flood any part of your being with awareness, and that it need not be an unconscious compulsion.

Starting again with the physical body, just quietly breathe for a few moments to place your awareness in the body. Feel your breath, in and out, rise and fall. Next, open your eyes, and through them, move your awareness out and "feel" whatever is in front of you. Feel the form of it and the space it occupies. Then close your eyes, and become aware of what is happening in your mind.

Pause.

When you feel your body with eyes closed, you have an inner awareness of your body and the physical life that your body experiences. When you open your eyes, you can feel your-self flowing from that inner awareness out into the world. These are tangible feelings, easily observed. But the third state, that of the mental and emotional, is harder to understand. Since it is composed of your mental and emotional awarenesses, it can feel chaotic and out of control, beyond your understanding. Whenever you are feeling angry, sad, jealous, anxious, judg-mental, and so on, you are in this state. Many of you think this third level is all there is to life, so you stay there. Instead of allowing it to become the only reality you know, you can move to a fourth state of awareness that we will call Beingness. *This is where you place your awareness on awareness itself.* How do you reach this fourth state? By becoming aware of the first three, and then asking, "What or who is aware of body, of world, of thoughts?" The more attention you pay to how these different states feel, the more comfortable and believable this fourth state of Beingness becomes. I am hoping, by the end of our present time together, you will all know that Beingness is as obvious an option of choice as the physical, manifest, and mental "realities" you have observed.

Much of yesterday's recording of "clusters" was the explo-ration of "three," referring to the third dimension. There are a multitude of feelings and thoughts in that state. The great danger in "three" is that it can distract you and lull you to sleep. When we practice moving into Beingness, the temptation of "three" is to have your mind take hold and try to understand *how* to get there, what it will *feel* like once you're there, *who else* says there is such a state, when to find time to *read up* on it, and how to find a *workshop* that will deepen your experience of it. In the end, all the wonderful glitter inherent in "threeness" will be overshadow-ing the possibilities of this fourth state of Beingness again. You invite this fourth dimension by admitting you don't have any idea of how to "get there." Then you simply let go, not even knowing if there *is* such a state of Beingness. Keep asking, "Who or what is this awareness? Who is aware of this awareness?" This is not something you do only once, but over and over again.

§ § §

So as the day progresses, be aware of what level you are on. If you are swimming in the water, you might be blissfully in the physical. Remember the wonderful feeling of just being in the body, without the mind chattering, without past or future concerns. And in the bliss of being in the physical, you might find yourself even more in Beingness. Watch what happens as you interact with other people, as your patterns and "clusters" assert themselves. The state of "threeness" is where the action is. It is where you are accustomed to getting the juice in your life, your feeling of being alive. But it is short-lived. The juice of Beingness is everlasting. The power of it is eternal. The power of Beingness is a state of joy and bliss, and that comes from the watchful awareness and total acceptance of the most incredible nonsense going on in "three." You don't have to clean up your mental-emotional body. You don't have to change it, fix it, or work on it. You can just choose to leave this state by slipping smoothly into Beingness, away from thought.

Please understand, this is just another way to illustrate choices. You have the ability to be aware of the Light of awareness wherever you choose. The Divine placed that gift in you, understanding that a state of "one," "two," or "threeness" goes on and on, and Beingness is *always* present. You can "Be" no matter how unloving, painful, or chaotic your world is at any moment. It does not have to be smiling, applauding, and cheering you on for you to stay in "four."

I don't care what you do with "three." There is enough "three" around to keep you going endlessly. It feeds on itself, but it can't get you off the ground and into Vastness. You can be caught up in the most magnificent love affair with another human being, and in the midst of it, wake up in the dark hours of the night with the loneliness still there. What I was hoping for in yesterday's exercise was a sense of observation, a sense that one could be in all of the circumstances of "threeness" and still get to that place of peace within. Several of you indicated there was something else present, but there was not yet a clear feeling of what that other was. Stay with the practice of awareness. Our job together is to find out what "it" is.

You can help yourself shift into Beingness by reminding yourself that it is always present. Even saying it in your mind will allow the magic of a transcendent power to drop you to that place. There's no way to trick yourself into it. You'll try all your tricks and end up saying, "I can't do it," and then it will happen. You'll try and repeat what you think got you there before, and it won't work, so again you'll say, "I can't," and again it will happen. *In the gaps between trying, Being happens.* So try. Try every way your ego wants you to, and then when you are tired, relax and watch. When you stop trying, it will be there. God is in the trying, and God is in the non-trying, in the seeking and in the finding.

It doesn't really matter what you do. In the midst of your forgetfulness, Beingness is there. It's always there. You are it. Slip into "three," but *watch* yourself slip. Thinking God thoughts in "three" is no different from thinking ungodly thoughts in "three." You may feel a little more holy thinking God thoughts and a little more guilty thinking the other, but neither has anything to do with the fact that "three" is "three," and both are "beingness."

Be observation Itself. Don't struggle. When you find yourself in the same kinds of mental, emotional drama, please don't say, "I don't want to be stuck here again. How do I get to 'four'?" That is the mind speaking. Just keep laughing, and then stop the static. When you say you don't know how, that is the biggest lie of all. You listen to "windbags" like me who are just trying to present you with more opportunities to make choices until you can know *you* are able to choose. Once you know you *can* choose, not *how* to choose, we are finished.

Are there any questions? No? Good, because any questions would come out of your mental-emotional "threeness." Just be willing to be the Creative Potential Itself. Let it have you. Create *some thing* and you miss it. Creation is not creating anything! *It is the feeling of the Creator Itself.* It does nothing and it goes nowhere, yet it goes everywhere and does everything, and I hope you are confused by the paradox. *There is nowhere to go, nothing to do.* It's all been done, and there was never anything "done," and I hope this is confusing enough to drop you into Beingness.

♪ ♪ ♪

Days Three and Four
Farther Out and Further In

Today I would like to see if we can bring together some of the frustrating fragments you experience in your awareness when different pieces of information don't seem to fit together. Frustration arises when there is no focused place of centering to which you can go to make an intuitive assessment about the truth of what you are hearing. That core place, that sense of being centered, is absolutely essential for you to be able to sense the truth of something. Without it, you will believe all kinds of lies about yourself. We want to stop the lies your world has been telling you.

Lies about yourself can take your energy and dissipate it in useless struggles that do not leave you in a state of love, not only for yourself, but for the moment you are living in. Our goal is to be in love with *the moment you are living in and nothing else.* The moment *itself!* This comes only when there is a place inside you that becomes home. That is a home where you go for truth, for love and comfort, delight and happiness. So this afternoon, I would like to speak about this "going home for truth" about yourself.

With all due respect, you have been told so many lies that you have lost knowledge of who you are and where that place of truth is. You no longer experience the "center" that can be relied upon to bring you data that is filled with truth. As a result, you go to what I would call secondary sources of information, sources containing an accumulation of knowledge, fact, and nonfact, and from them believe what you are told. You believe what you see, you believe what you hear, and you believe what you hear about *yourself*. I am asking you to break down that belief system, to destroy it; because out of the destruction of lies, truth is left.

All aspects of God-Awareness are located in that center, and it is the only place you can count on to reflect God's wisdom. It is the only place you can go to answer the question, "What does God think of me?" However spiritually sophisticated you get, the double-edged question remains, "Is there a God?" and "What does that God think of me?" One of the reasons you run away from finding out the answer to the first question is because you live in terror of the answer to the second.

§ § §

The capacity for exuberant young children to find God is infinite. They can honestly believe there is such a thing as a loving, compassionate, beautiful God out there just for them. But when rules and regulations arise, as they do in every organized religion and society, they bring with them fear and guilt. You work against yourselves because of this fear and guilt. Should you come to that place of knowing there is a God, then follows the incredible terror of what that God thinks about you.

In these years, in my own way, I have tried to show you how God really feels about you. I have revealed what God's essence is and how the Divine knows who and what you are. But nevertheless, the fact remains that I haven't entirely convinced some of you who have been with us these 12 years. I haven't convinced you because I *cannot* convince you. If I could, I would have done it 12 years ago and left, because there would be nothing else to say. That knowledge is not transferable. It is the kind of *experiential data* you have to accumulate for yourself. In my work with you, I set up the circumstances that continue building the power that will then allow you to have the experience. I can create the availability, but you create the willingness. These are just words right now, but I am using them to build a space where you will be willing to risk what God thinks of you. I want to push you to that place where you will say, "I need to know. I am willing to risk knowing because not knowing is too painful." Not knowing becomes so uncomfortable that the only way out is in finding out if God exists and what God thinks of you.

That's all this is about—*to remember what you already know, and to give you a moment to experience that which you already are.* Nothing fancy, nothing magical, just ordinary God-Consciousness. Ordinary because that's just what it is. When you become aware of your connection with the Divine, you will realize you have been feeling it forever, and you will be amazed that you have gone so long without remembering or acknowledging what it is you were feeling. You will become aware it has been there all along and nothing has changed, yet everything has changed. It's one of those magical times, and the magic is you and this moment.

It is my contention that, should you choose, any of you can touch that center so strongly and make the journey to it so easy that you will view more and more of your world from that place within. And when life becomes painful or chaotic, you will be so grounded that you will understand exactly what I am talking about when I say, "home" is where you must live. As you have this experience again and again, you will begin to believe it. You

will finally touch upon and acknowledge the totality of the inno-
cence and belief in your own pure consciousness. All lies then
quiet down. I can't attack the lies. I have consistently told you
that you are absolutely beautiful, you have done nothing wrong,
you are perfect and marvelous just as you are, and you are totally loved. And you say, "Thank you," and go home and forget it.
So it doesn't do any good to talk about it. The only thing that's
going to win the victory is your own experience.

$ $ $

Please hear this. *You are already experiencing that experience!* That is the statement you hang on to. It is the place you
keep going back to. When your mind begins to deflect you with
other ideas, beliefs, stories, and dramas, remember what I have
just said. *You are already fully experiencing,* not God, just fully
experiencing! If I say "experience God," it is a lie. There are not
two things. There isn't experience and God; there is just experience. And in the experience *is* God. You begin to talk about it,
and immediately you are one step away from it. Do you see the
paradox? If you think about the experience, you lose it, but if
you don't think about experiencing, you can't bring it to your
awareness.

Are you experiencing? Of course you are! You *all* are! *Then
you are enlightened!* If you have to, run it as a mantra. "I am
Enlightened." It must be ingrained in you. There is a part of you
that receives all data and makes decisions based on that data.
When you program that part of you with one consistent thing, it
forms a belief. If one person, one moment, one day said, "You are
an idiot!" and you never heard it again, you would forget it. But if
it is repeated again and again, you will believe it, not because it's
true, but because it's been repeated so often. Repetition doesn't
make truth, but it certainly makes something sound convincing.
So why not repeat the truth—*you are already experiencing the*

feeling you are looking for. Repeat it to yourself constantly, no matter what the mind tells you.

What about the so-called bad experiences? Look at what you are now discovering. People in the midst of the most incredible guilt, fear, or sorrow can drop to that place where they embrace the experience of grief, loss, or fear. This does not mean that they enjoy the emotion, but they are willing to stay with it and move to a deeper level, to the core of the feeling, being willing to experience it fully. They find the "God" in the guilt, fear, or sorrow. There is an important distinction here. Your identification with trying to make your life happy to avoid unhappiness is where your ego has got you by the throat. You get rid of the difficulties with your children or your spouse or your jobs, but the addiction to *trying to feel good* remains. This is where you are caught. I know this is difficult, but stay with me. Don't talk about it, don't intellectualize it, just remember, *"I am already experiencing what I am looking for,"* and then stop and wait. What happens? Test it. Realize what's at stake here. Knowing you are already experiencing your enlightenment convinces the part of you that is the seeker to stop seeking. When you ask, "How do I move from the seeker to the finder?" we are caught again. We are back in the words. The mind is going to play with you, thinking up more exciting words, more beautiful words to describe the experience you are looking for. And in the end, the words will make you the perpetual seeker.

So you need to settle down into the inner silence, and the technique we use for that is usually called "staying with the moment, with what is here, now." You are going to get bored. You are going to get ecstatic. You are going to get everything in-between. Just stay with it. Stay with whatever is being presented. I am hoping you will come to know you can begin to build this intensity no matter what you are doing. You can't all sit in closets for the rest of your life, meditating. It's time to be able to *do* and to *be* at the same time. Remember, the delight of being in a human body is that you can act on it, through it, and with it.

I would like to ask you to sit still right now, wherever you are, for a 15-minute silent round of meditation. Begin by remembering this simple directive: **Watch your breath.** *First thing into the body, watch your breath. Be aware of breath as life rising and falling. The minute you do that, you place yourself deeply inside your body, which is where the experience of God-Consciousness is felt. You are* **already feeling it,** *because as we have agreed, you are all experiencing.*

Feel how quiet you can become when you are like the cat waiting at the mouse hole. The cat is waiting, not for the mouse, but for the experience of cat-ness. The ego says to watch for the mouse, and I say, forget the mouse. The mouse is on the other side waiting to feel mouse-ness. It's that kind of intense, yet relaxed, gentle, but totally focused feeling you're looking for. And to get it, keep silent and watch what happens.

Pause.

Stop and consider a moment how humorous it is to think that it's difficult to be yourself. Isn't this a strange concept to believe you have to struggle to become conscious of what you already are? You *are* the still center point. You don't have to make it. You don't have to grope around to find it. There is no special button to push in order to have it. The wonderful thing about God is there's no off switch. It always works at the same rate of power and consistency. How you choose to experience the Divine may vary, but the power does not. This is why I can say with absolute truth: *You are all created equal.*

Day Five

Who Says "Who Am I," When I Ask, "Who Am I"?

Yesterday we briefly discussed the necessity to reintroduce, to bring to your attention, truths that you already know. There are no surprises. Nothing ever said by any energy that comes from the Heart of God should really surprise you. So nothing "new" is being created, just eternal principles being remembered.

With that in mind, I would like to reintroduce you to the Experiencer, that part of yourself that watches everything going on in your body, mind, environment, and life, collecting vast amounts of data. It is possible to watch your thoughts as they rise and fall and to become aware of *who or what it is* that is doing this watching. The awareness that watches simply keeps asking, "Who is seeing this? Who is hearing this? Who is feeling this?" always going back to the "Who." When you drop back to asking "Who is," do not answer the question. You do not say, "I am," because it will then create another question, which is, who is this "I" that is you? You can't answer this with your mind because *your mind doesn't know.* You don't know *who* you are when you try to describe yourself. And on a deeper level, you know exactly who or what you are. You are just pretending to be asleep to that knowledge, and so we are trying to gently awaken you to it once again.

As you quiet yourself down by experiencing your own center without thought, you can feel an increase or "rise" in the energy within you. And as you continue to push toward that deeper level by asking, "Who is experiencing this energy?" you also create an inner tension. The energy builds, and a feeling of inner tension builds as well. Who is experiencing both the tension and the increase in energy? Don't stop with just feeling it. Take the next step. Keep asking the question that turns it back on itself. All kinds of obstacles will rise. The way out, the way through them, is to keep asking, "Who is experiencing this doubt, this confusion, this boredom?" The tendency is to move away from the Experiencer and begin to analyze, think, and focus again on that which is being experienced.

§ § §

So let's increase the tension a bit here and get closer to the experience. This exercise may be difficult for some of you, but please trust that it will be helpful. Get yourselves a sheet of paper and a pen or pencil. Then sit quietly and take a few moments to think of some event that has already happened that you didn't like. It can be something you have done, something about yourself you don't like, a circumstance that has happened to you, or anything in your life that is or has been unpleasant.

*Reexperience that event. Make it very real through visualization, memory, emotional responses, or anything that helps. As you reexperience the feelings of the unpleasant event, **listen to the messages your ego is giving you.** What thoughts do you have about what is going on? What you are looking for might best be described as "diabolical one-liners." They are things like, "I never can do anything right," or "You are a bad person because you left your children," or "People can't be trusted to be good to me."*

Write down all the one-liners that come out of that event. As you do, you will begin to feel others surfacing as well. Place all of them somewhere on your paper. This will give you a very clear picture of what messages your ego constantly bombards you with, without you being aware of them. These are the messages that you believe reflect the "real you."

Pause until finished.

You run your lives on such negative mantras—mantras that are lies, but are so deeply embedded in you that you honestly believe they are you. As an example, your one-liner might be, "I am too slow!" It may run your life. In response to that idea, true or untrue, you may find that you walk too fast, you talk too fast, everything you do is too fast; and it's because you keep hearing the complaint from your past that you are too slow. This may not be such a detriment in the physical world, but every one of these negative mantras presents a spiritual obstacle. In this case, the belief that "I'm too slow" prevents this person from just being who they are. They practice slowing down by becoming aware of the mantras driving them. "Do more. Do it better. Do it faster." Where are you going so quickly? Being driven by this one-liner is not going to help anyone "find God" any sooner. What will help is to sit down, be still, and relax. Stop feeling like you have to do it all, and just be. Identify what it is inside you that keeps telling you that you have to be something else. This is a conditioned world that tells you that that kind of feeling—that joy, that wonder, that bliss of just being who you are, is somehow not enough.

So please, look again at the statements you have written down. Some of them will touch you more deeply than others. Look at them in light of what we have just said. How does this lie about you keep you from your goal of knowing you are an Enlightened Being? This is an opportunity to see how these lies continue to move you in directions that block that experience. These one-liners keep you on the move, keep you from being relaxed. I have told you over and over again, relaxation is the key to allowing yourself the pleasure of experience. Your conditioned beliefs about yourself are what produce the tensions in your life. They are the places you drift to in your consciousness a hundred times a day. And in the drifting, you begin to worry. While I am saying, sit down and be quiet, there's nowhere to go anyway, half of you say, "Oh, good," and the other half say, "I don't believe it." Don't underestimate the power of your underlying beliefs, my friends. The thing that keeps the whole spiritual game going is the tension created by these lies.

Question: If we stop caring about whether we do good, look good, or are loving or rich, when it's all gone, what's left?

What is yours to live through and with will continue to be there, but the anxiety will be gone. It will *all* be there, but the anxiety will be gone. The tension will be released, and in your relaxation, you will begin to *feel* your beauty, *sense* your goodness, and *know* your life is full of what you need. You are in charge of what you focus your awareness on. So, as you go about this day, practice looking out for your destructive one-liners. When you hear one, stop and let yourself fully hear it and feel it. Then pull your awareness away from "all that," and drop into the Experiencer. You can easily do this by asking, "Who is experiencing all that?" Stay with this feeling until you bump up against another negative mantra. If you repeat this process over and over, by the end of the day, you will *know* you can shift the awareness of what you pay attention to. At the same time, you will have begun to replace the lies about yourself with the truth of who you are. When you are just experiencing, without thought, what you experience is your wonder, power, and beauty. Do not say you can't tell the difference between your ego and God. That is the greatest lie of all. God feels unconditionally wonderful, that's how you tell. Tension of any kind tells you that ego is present.

$$\emptyset\ \emptyset\ \emptyset$$

It is one thing to sit quietly in a workshop situation practicing this, but quite another thing happens when you are participating in the world of your senses. Most of the time you lose the experience of what you tap into. What you want is to be able to live life as life presents itself every moment, and to be aware of and able to move into the part of you that is experiencing it. In truth, you are doing this all the time. You have an idea that there is a "you" doing this thing called "living life." No! *The Source is doing everything, and if the Source is doing everything, then should you not be able to experience the Source at the same time that you are doing anything?* The idea that the Source is one thing and you and your life are something else is a belief that needs to die.

It takes commitment, willingness, and the yearning to know that there is no separation between you and the Divine to persevere in what you call "the search for God." Most of all, it takes practice to convince yourself that God or Awareness Itself is real and is present NOW. You believe that you rise up out of Source, leave Source behind, and move into your life. What I am trying to show you is that you never leave the Source, which is the Essence of who you are—never!

The ego has been trying to convince you that paying close enough attention to its voice will somehow guarantee that you can get what it says you want. "Play by my rules and I will make you happy," says the ego. "I will show you how to impress other people. I will teach you how to make people love and admire you. I will see to it that you are important and special. All these things will be yours when you pay attention to me." Well, you have been doing this for a long time. Has it worked? Are you important enough? Are you happy enough? Have you really achieved enough specialness to satisfy the ever-gnawing desire of the ego? If you are willing to be the Experiencer of Essence in the midst of *anything*, you will be able to laugh at the inflated importance of your own repertoire. And the ego wants you to do anything but have a good belly laugh about "all that stuff." Just the act of laughing at your own grand assortment of ego clichés will help you release them.

So for today, just practice being the experiencer of Essence every moment. Since you are *always* experiencing Essence, because you are Essence Itself, you are already doing what I am asking, only you are not aware of it. The experience contains the Essence. The mystery of Enlightenment, the mystery of this process of finding God, lies right here. The Bible says, "Seek and ye shall find." "Be still and know." That's the job, over and over again; seek and ye shall find, *be still and know.* I am not asking you to do something hard or painful. I am asking you to do what you are already doing and to *be aware of what is in the experience.* Pay attention to the incredible trivia that keeps you from it. It's just silly material that runs you around in the same circles. "I didn't get what I wanted." "Pay more attention to me." "That hurt my feelings." Endless nonsense. But behind it all is the pearl without price, the Light everlasting, Compassion unending, the live knowledge of the magnificent wonder of your Being.

Every time you are ready to fight for your rights, ask yourself this very simple question. *Do you want to be number one, or do you want to be One?* Those are the two choices, *to be number one or to be One.* Feeling the Essence of your Self helps you make the choice to be One without giving up anything. Don't trade it for being right. Don't trade it for being smart or beautiful or wealthy. Don't trade it and don't give it away. Whatever experience you are having right now *is it!*

§ § §

Day Six
No Matter Why You Came, Enlightenment Is Your Game

I would like to talk to those of you who, after yesterday's work, are having difficulty acknowledging that you are Essence. Some of you have uncovered painful things about yourselves, and others of you have become aware of how much of life is run by unconscious one-liners. This kind of inward journey is called a birthing exercise because it does involve pain. There is a part in all of you that has spent lifetimes trying to rid yourselves of emotional pain by projecting it out onto other people or by simply refusing to feel it. Some of you are still skittering

on the edge of wanting to believe that "everything is fine," even
though what you are really feeling is terrible. You refuse to
acknowledge the seeming paradox. "How can it be that all is
Light and Love, and yet I am in pain?"

For those of you who feel this, the challenge is to reconcile
the presence of the Divine and the presence of pain. You have
been taught that God represents the absence of painful events in
your lives. So if there is pain, there is no God. That is simply not
so! You can reconcile this dilemma by allowing yourself the full
experience of the painful feeling and then simply ask, "Who is
feeling this?" At first your ego will struggle and try to get you
back into thinking about it by trying to answer with a mental
statement. I ask you to use *all the power of your awareness* to
keep going back to the "Who?" It is your way to clarity.

You cannot feel God-Awareness until you allow yourself to
feel, without preference, whatever is present in any moment. You
are afraid to feel fully because you are afraid your inner pain will
overwhelm you. But when you focus your awareness on that
pain, you will begin to feel that something besides pain is also
present. You become aware of the reality that it does not matter
what you are feeling, because that awareness is present in all feeling, and is feeling it all. Let's test this.

$ $ $

Start by paying attention to your breathing. When you have
settled into your body, let a feeling float into your awareness.
Don't scurry around mentally, trying to find something specific.
Just sit quietly and let it come. It will rise up in you naturally—
some feeling associated with a memory, thought, or event. If it is
an event, look at it and get the feeling you had when the event
took place. When that is clearly present, hold it; and, at the same
time, keep a very careful watch for what else is present. No mat-

ter what feeling is present, something else is there, also. Just see if you can find that now.

Pause.

I repeat, if you are not in touch with your feelings, how are you going to feel God? Are you willing to risk feeling pain in order to feel God? Yes or no? The idea that you have to get rid of painful feelings before you can feel the Divine is not true. In the end, this is simply a course in choosing what you want to be aware of at any moment. You are here to learn this so you can decide whether you want to be happy or sad; whether you want to feel safety or fear, anxiety or peace. You have this one choice. If you do not know that, then when the winds of life blow, you will just have to wait for them to subside. Standing in the wind, baking in the sun, and being in pain can be blissful when you understand you have a choice. The choice is not between one object or another, one location or another, one desire or another. The choice is to stay with what is happening, to let it play fully on you, and thereby begin to experience *all* that is present. God is in that All.

§ § §

When you ask, "What am I here for?" I say, to become aware of Who you really are, not who your mind tells you that you are. I ask you to see this as your job. In addition to that, do other things. Maybe get a degree in therapy so you can help people or have six children or run a business. But if you really have a commitment to this, then consider it to be your primary job. It is important to talk about this because I think you forget the incredible defeats and victories that go with any job. You do not expect to come home every day with a radiant smile on your face or undying love in your heart after working eight hours. You understand that things go up and down. Some people will frown, and some people will smile. You expect that. But when it comes to this job of discovering your true nature, you expect only Light and Love, peace and beauty.

In working toward this, things will come and go just like any other job. Sometimes you win and sometimes you lose. Some days are clear, some days are foggy, and some days are totally rained out. But your focus remains the same. You are not here to publish books, you are here to become aware of WHO does all that is done on this Earth plane. As an aside, you publish books. As an aside, you run a corporation or work in a drive-in. But the sooner you begin to use all hours of the day for your real job, the easier you will make it.

So make the inner statement, "Awakening to Awareness is my 24-hour-a-day job." If you don't, you will forget about it, and then if you have time, you will meditate. Then if you have time, you will relax into Essence. And then if you have time, you will be loving and kind. I am asking you to reverse this. If you have time, get a job. If you have time, make some money. If you have time, get married. If you have time, raise children. But you will never reach the goal until you understand that *Awakening to the Now is the job!* Get a clear understanding of what each day is for, and everything will move more quickly.

You ask, "How can you tell me Awakening is my primary aim when I have so many other important things going on in my life?" Let us say you are working for a large corporation. You know it is important to keep your humor and to be effective and positive about yourself and everything that's going on around you, to make sure your work is done in the allotted time. You are doing many, many different things as you walk through your nine-to-five job, but the one central focus is the same—to do the job well so you will get the recognition you are working for. Now, say that your central focus is not personal recognition, but Awakening. With that focus, you will be able to find endless ways to remember this. As you go about the many different aspects of your day, you can surely find ways to maximize and further your job of finding the Light, just as you found ways to maximize your chances of recognition in your job.

Everything you do can further the process. Then ripeness will come, and you will fall into the arms of God. All of life partakes of the ripening process, and some of it is pleasing and uplifting, and some of it is just plain painful. Nothing springs from the ground already producing flowers and fruit. This is a process of growth. If the objective of your life is this Awakening, then look for ways to awaken in everything you do. Keep participating in the ripening, and thank God that some day it will all be very clear, and you will be fully aware of that state called "Filled with Light."

⚶ ⚶ ⚶

Day Seven
Closing the Circle

A very creative psychic named Jane Roberts has done some excellent work that is transformative on the deepest level. She brought forward a concept that many people are quoting in many contexts. Her statement is that you create your own reality. Becoming aware of what is meant by this will enable you to watch your life as various things come into form, dissolve, and are then recreated in other forms.

You can truly create your reality—not only in the physical sense, but in other dimensions as well. Thought is another dimension in which you create. You create thoughts all the time, and these thoughts create your world. When you don't like a thought or belief, you can stop creating it in its present form, and create another to take its place. The difficulty comes when you believe the thoughts you create are universal truths. With them, you create a belief filter. These filters determine what you will allow yourself to see and hear. They provide just one interpretation of your experiences. Other interpretations may be as interesting and more expansive and helpful, but you can't see or hear them. This can change when you have a willingness to see every thought, every event, and every interaction as simply coming from one limited point of view. This point can change if you are willing.

Just because beliefs are part of large religious or intellectual structures *does not make them true.* If you are addicted to holding on to your "truth" or your reality or your view of the world or your belief about God or good health or relationships or philosophy or money, that is what you are stuck with. This is very small thinking. As Dr. Serge King says, "If it works, it's true!" Think about that for a minute. If it works for you, it's your truth. If it works, don't fix it. This is much closer to universal truth and a key to creating your own reality.

Thoughts also give birth to your emotions. The thought comes first, and then the emotion arises. *Any emotion created by the ego alone has limits because you are using the limitations of the ego to create it.* So your most horrendous feeling, fantasy, or fear *has a limit to it.* And everything that is limited can be gotten rid of. Emotions such as fear, anger, grief, or judgment can be removed if you so desire.

If you are two inches tall and you see a 10,000-foot wave coming at you, your first response would be, "Get me out of here!" That is sometimes how you feel in the face of your strong emotions. The small, frightened, childlike part of you responds like this because "life" looked so overwhelming to you when you were little. But it does not have to be like that. You are not little. You are vast. It's time to quit pretending you are small. Quit pretending you are so afraid. Quit pretending and become aware of what's happening by staying with your fears. Experience them fully. Don't run. Remember you are vast, with infinite resources, and the capability to overcome whatever you want and need to. You are not the victim of your life.

You are the 10,000-foot wave, as well as those feelings two inches high. Your real Essence, your real strength, your reservoir of potential possibility, change, and extension is a 10,000-foot wave. This fearful feeling or remembrance of a past event that's not even here anymore is just a fragment that drifts in and out of that vastness. The fragment comes and goes. It is not permanent. And as you watch this coming and going of negative emotions, you will get the direct experience that you are not that fear. It is something that enters "you" and then exits. So pay close attention. This is where you will learn control over your own consciousness.

You have endless choices and flexibility within conscious-ness. You can visualize the painful event or feeling with a differ-ent outcome, or see yourself no longer weak and helpless, but strong and capable. You can also choose to feel an expanded state of awareness and look at the entire situation from another per-spective. An idea like, "What will this look and feel like in ten years? Five years?" might help. Remember, you are the 10,000-foot wave!

It is a lie that thoughts are something eternal, enduring, and unchangeable. *If you are not thinking a certain thought, then it is not a part of your reality.* Let us say that someone close to you died yesterday, but you couldn't be reached with that informa-tion. You have been going along having a wonderful time, swim-ming in the afternoon, socializing with your friends, and enjoy-ing life. Then you find out about the death, and suddenly you are in terrible despair. But you weren't yesterday when the event took place. You were fine until you learned about it. The event hap-pened, and the death was real. But your pain started when the thought, *I've lost someone,* entered your mind. The vast part of you, the wave, knows you haven't really lost anything. Just the form has changed. It is the mind that brought the fear and pain. So try to remember that there is a vast part of you that knows "all's well" even in the face of such experiences. There is valuable information in this illustration.

You can change your ideas of pain, suffering, and limitation by remembering this process. Just as you brought one idea in, you can bring others in and leave others out. Whatever is current in your mind seems real. *Out of sight, out of mind. Out of mind, out of reality.* If you are not thinking it, if you are not aware of it, at that moment it is not real. This is important. Any painful, unacceptable, inappropriate, or overwhelming feeling, idea, thought, or belief about an event that is not happening this moment can be reduced to nothing by the feeling of the 10,000-foot wave.

Concentrate on what you wish to have in your life. What you concentrate on, you make real, you make manifest. If you are inundated with difficult feelings, you now know you have the capability to create expansive ones. It's your *reluctance* to let go of the negative feelings that keeps you trapped! Drop them out of your mind. Realize *you* are creating them; *you are doing this to yourself.* Your past cannot trap you unless you let it. Drop the past and be here now. Then you can learn the delight and joy of just stepping out into a different frequency. Step into something else, and in so doing, leave the past behind. When you choose to step into peace, into joy, into compassion, you enter something new and different. And from that new and different place, you can quietly allow the past to dissolve.

This week I have asked you to stop and really feel your pain. The minute you slow the process down and begin to look at it, you become aware that there is also something or someone watching the pain, something or someone thinking about the pain. Who or what is that? From this place of observation, you will come to know you are the 10,000-foot wave, and the thing you are looking at is two inches tall.

§ § §

I would like to end as I began. It is the "I" of your ever-present awareness that gets vast in meditation. It is the vast "I" that sees problems rising and falling and accepts them as transitory. It is the "I" that sees the Light and is the Light. It is the witness, the observer. It is that which *never changes,* that which watches the whole process. However much we talk about changing concepts and emotions and moving to other beliefs, none of that stands as important beside one basic knowing. You are the Self. You have never been anything but the Self. It is the Self that illumines everything. The Self *is.* Stay with the Self, and the rest is done. Move out of that Self, and the 10,000 things arise. Return to the Self, and they dissolve. Every moment is as perfect in the Self as the next.

There is only one Truth that is knowable, and that is the Truth of who you are. Who is it that sees and feels the pain? Who is it that decides to expand and have delight and joy in its life? Who is it that drives the car? Who is it that eats, sleeps, and loves? *Who are you? What are you?* That is the only question. It is the most knowable of all things, because it is already happening. All of it is happening in the Self, as the Self.

There is nothing wrong. There is nothing right. There is nothing to learn. There is nothing to find. There is nothing to let go of. You are life, and Life is God, and God is All. Nothing is outside of God—nothing. So hold to that and be free.

You cannot feel
God-Awareness
until you allow
yourself to feel,
without preference,
whatever is present
in any moment.

PART II

Journey

4
A Brother's Gift

I have often told you that this communication we share between us is an experiment in consciousness. Certain energies on "our side of the Light" have begun and continued this undertaking with the expectation and hope that parts of this so-called invisible reality could enter your world and increase your experience of the Grace of God-Consciousness. We bring this idea forward in as many ways as we can, to let you know that the main component of consciousness is what you would call Grace, the Love of God, the total experience of acceptance from the God-Source.

§ § §

Our desire was to have this teaching encourage the physical body to feel the presence of this Grace in the midst of any physical extremity or illness of body, mind, or emotion. It was hoped you would allow yourself to experience this Divine acceptance awash in your body and ablaze in your consciousness, no matter what else was taking place. We wished to help you move away from an old model of consciousness that said you must stop feeling what you were feeling, whether sinful, ill, angry, unbalanced, jealous, or whatever "negative" emotion was present. The new model would help you realize it is not the way of the Divine to *remove* all of the negative experiences from your lives, but to show you a way to feel them, freely and completely, and then move on to a feeling that was more to your liking.

Individual destiny could be said to be "true" in the linear, limited sense, but it is not all of your life, and it is not the only experience possible in your life. Whatever may be going on with your health, with your bank accounts, with your love affairs, and with your jobs are all examples of linear occupations. The hope was that our coming together for these years would stimulate a remembrance that the Grace and Love of God is also present in each of these events and is not something very vague or far removed. It was hoped that you would allow yourselves, on an ongoing basis, to feel it.

So, have we been successful? Oh yes. And why? Because you have kept coming to these gatherings in spite of your doubts. Many of you didn't fully believe in this energy called Bartholomew in 1977, and continued to have doubts over the passing years, yet you came, you sat, you listened, you hoped and you prayed. In other words, you stayed with it. Without your willingness to hear this teaching, no matter how strange the format, we would not have been able to change the basic imagery you have constructed about your world or your idea of who you are and who God is. To say that success is possible because of our side of the light is to misspeak it. The success is because of you. It comes from your constant, ongoing presence in the face of personal confusion and doubt, self-doubt as well as doubt about the entire process. Stop and think of what has happened to you in these years we have shared together. It has been an ongoing motion between belief and doubts.

Your victory is in your willingness to hear or read these words and stay open to them in the midst of doubt, confusion, disbelief, or disapproval. I know there has been a certain amount of disruption in your lives from following this path. Some people have lost their marriages and the approval of family and friends. But that willingness to keep holding on to the possibility of discovering there is no separation between God and self, and the willingness to stay and allow the motion of that energy to move through you is where we have all been successful. There is a mutuality in this gift. While we have given to you, please know that you have also given back.

Look back and think about the first time you heard these words, and reflect upon where you are now and how you feel about yourself and your connection to God, and you will realize you are not the same—and you will never be the same. You are the forerunners of a new way of approaching consciousness. This teaching has to be grounded and run through physical bodies. It cannot just be thrown out into the ethers. It hasn't happened before because you were not ready to listen, to suffer your doubts, or to allow this kind of experience to begin a process. You weren't ready, and the moment enough of you were, the experiment began.

$$\textdollar \; \textdollar \; \textdollar$$

In the year 1977, this was seen as a very strange kind of happening. Something was said to move through this human vehicle and a so-called spiritual teaching came out. The presentation was thought to be unusual and different. Now it is very commonplace, is it not? Things have been changing rapidly, and while this approach is valid now, this kind of presentation will eventually end because *it will no longer be needed.* Since the announcement a few months ago that this entire verbal, public experiment will end no later than 1995, the question has been "Why?" There are many reasons, but at a very basic level, it is because God does not waste time, and this kind of "transmitting" of a spiritual teaching will become less necessary as you awaken to this awareness yourself.

As you move away from the belief in "me" as an external "something" and begin to understand that this energy is a part of you, as it is Mary-Margaret, you will begin to experience it *for yourself.* You will become so intimate with it that you will just sit in the quietness of your own knowing, and the answers to your questions will come in an immediate, direct way. I have asked all of you who are interested in your own self-enlightenment to spend time in these next years strengthening your experience that this energy you call Bartholomew *is you.*

If the world only mirrors back what you are, then what am I? Is this Bartholomew phenomenon so distant that it does not reflect back in your mirror, or is it a reminder that those attributes you give to me are a part of you? If you have ever heard or read these words, or been present at any sharing of them, and if you acknowledge the world as mirror, then this awareness must also be you. I am not separate. I am not a gift to Mary-Margaret just for her own use that then comes to you from her. This consciousness is a mirror of you. It is the potential for *all* of consciousness, and you will see it repeated again and again. You must realize, the purpose of this is not for some chosen few to experience this energy, but to begin a *process* for as many of you as possible. What process? The process of unfolding the connection between us. You have the power to know where the truth lies, to know where the Light is, and the ability to be those things. That is the job. I am the mirror.

When you know that you are a part of the whole, of the All, as "I" am, any fear of my leaving will immediately disappear. Any anxiety that I am going to leave you in any kind of abandonment will no longer be a threat. You will come to know that *you*, in this moment, *are all of it!* If all is God, then I am God and you are God and this is the understanding you *must* come to. Any consciousness that has been present in any human form at all is a mirror available for you. Any wise and true statement you have ever read, heard, or intuited about someone else who is a human is here for your use. Anything anyone has done, positive or negative, is also possible for you. It is one vast, whole mirror of consciousness and there is nothing outside of that mirror. All appearances come and go in that mirror, and the mirror remains untouched by what is reflected in it. There are no favorite images, none.

$$\text{\musDoubleSharp}\ \text{\musDoubleSharp}\ \text{\musDoubleSharp}$$

On the material plane, do you wish to know about acquiring money? Are there millionaires in the world? Yes. That's all you need to know. Have there been great, enlightened ones? Yes. Then you too can be enlightened. The reason you don't get your share of the pie, whether materially or spiritually, is because you believe you can't have it. These beliefs are guaranteed to keep you separate from that which you seek. Any reflection of some-one who has what you think you are lacking can remind you that, if they have it, you can, too. If you want money, begin to focus on the tremendous amount of abundance in the world, and allow yourself to feel that abundance unspecified, is also flowing through you. Welcome this knowing.

As you focus on this knowing, remember that there is really no lack anywhere because you are not an individual seeking something you do not have, but the vast Being of Awareness, which contains everything within it. Just allow yourself to expe-rience the truth that you have everything you need—always.

You use the same process to feel abundance as you do to be one with God. There is no difference. If you say looking for money is separate from looking for God, you may never have either. Please hear this: *There is no money without God. The power of money is God in action.* Don't separate any of it, my friends. God is the yearning to have an empowered way of being in the world so that one feels one is doing what one wants to do. That is God in action. God sells books. God runs a computer. God teaches. God learns. God loves children. God creates beauty. God drives a truck. God helps others. God is. Don't separate. The minute you separate, you lose power. Hear this as deeply as you can. Whatever you yearn for, whatever face it is taking, it is God. If you yearn for a home of your own, that's God. That's a prayer. Your yearnings for a home are not what you think they are. They reflect the yearning for a home within. *All* your desires are prayers. They may be prayers on different levels of consciousness, but they are still prayers. Fear is a prayer, guilt is a prayer, and dissatisfaction is a prayer.

Start getting delighted by the fact that you have yearnings, that you experience disappointment, that you feel frustration. When you start rejoicing that you want things *because you know what they really mean,* you are on your way. Fully accept what you now desire, and you later will desire something vaster. Don't stop your desires, just take them as a reminder that if you do not feel complete, that if there is something you need, then be grateful for the reminder that what you really want is to go Home. Seeking for anything is seeking for God, only it is disguised as seeking for something else.

You say you never want to have any fear at all. But fear, however difficult, is like a bell going off to remind you why you are really fearful. You have a fight with a loved one or can't make your house payment, and you think that is why you're upset. It may seem that way, but the fear reminds you that you are feeling limited. The fight will end, and the house may or may not get paid for, but these are limited miseries and will pass. When they do, you are left with the realization that you still do not feel complete. You feel miserable because you feel separate—you want God. The minute you say that to yourself, the part of you waiting for this connection lights up.

Keep reminding yourself that the real pain, the real loneliness, the real fear, is not because you are separate from money or lovers or jobs, but because you feel yourself to be separate from God. Then simply ask, "Help me. I am afraid. I am afraid that my search for you will never end. Please help me to know Who You Are." Don't try to change anything. Just see these things for what they are, signals of the real dilemma. In that moment of realization, those external, small problems become less important. Your real desire can be fulfilled. With God, all things are possible.

Are there any questions?

$ $ $

Bartholomew, when I first met you , I asked the question, "Who are you?" and you answered, "Figure that out and the game is up." So, the question is, who are you? And the answer is, me.

That is correct. You all know it, but you don't *know* it. Throughout this experiment, we have been stating again and again, there is only One. If you are in the presence of Bartholomew, this energy is also you, not in some abstract sense, but in reality. You are you, and you are the person next to you and the one down the block. I want you to bang your brains against this statement. Get behind it and get to the truth that lies deeply below it. It is the koan of consciousness. How can it be that there is only One, when things seem to be so separate? There is a part of you that doesn't even want to know. So the answer to your question is a question. Who or what is the "I"? I will say it again. My awareness is your awareness. There is no separation. We are not two *pretending* to be one, we *are* one. We are One, pretending to be two! That is the game of Life.

You need to know in what way and in what part of your own being you experience this "me and you" as "just one thing." You no longer believe that the silent observation of yourself and your world will bring enlightenment. You think verbalization makes things real, yet every time I speak, I am stepping *down* the energy in order to verbalize. Understanding through speech alone is not possible. *You understand through experiencing.* So I ask you to quit the verbalization and the mentalization and use the next years we come together to come to an understanding of how I am you.

Those of you who love Bartholomew, whatever it represents, please use this as a mantra. Repeat to yourself: "I have to *know* it is me so I will not have one moment of sorrow, one moment of grief, one moment of fear of separation that I think is coming." Peace of heart will be there the moment you know you and this energy are the same. Throw yourself into *this* desire instead of into lesser things. How much do you want to know? Ask, "How can that energy and I be one?" The moment you will know it is the moment that all of this makes *internal, experiential sense.* In your body you will feel the Oneness. And with that feeling, everything changes.

It's a simple process, but it has to be all-consuming. If you are not interested in finding out your connection to my awareness, find out what God-Awareness is. What is this God that everyone keeps talking about? What does It feel like? You can go to therapy for the next hundred and fifty years with the finest therapist that ever lived, and you will still be lonely and miserable until you find the God within you. Yes, of course, take care of your external life. This is not an either/or path, but please understand that *you cannot expect a limited action to answer the cry of the soul.*

I promise that every time you turn your awareness, however confused, however limited, to this yearning to know, *I will be there.* That is a promise not only to those of you in this room, but to anyone who either sees or hears this who has the intention of attaining that goal. The goal is not unreachable. The answer must come. That is why you have undertaken this journey, so let's do it. Don't pretend to know you are a being full of Light pretending to be a body. If you *knew* that, you would not experience one moment of anything other than peace. So, if you don't experience ongoing peace, don't think you know, and don't let your mind trick you. Stop thinking. Start allowing.

Doubt is everywhere, and that is what you have to push against. The ego uses doubt to convince you that God-Awareness is not real. When you listen to all the people who tell you it can't be true, it reinforces the doubt within you. You must push against it. Just keep saying, "I want to know," as many moments of every day as you can. When you find yourself upset at someone, or angry at life itself, go ahead, but remember that the cause is not what it appears to be. You are not angry or upset or lonely or frightened for the reasons you think you are. *You are not!* There is something much, much deeper and much more terrifying going on than the feeling that you might not get what you want in the physical manifestations of your life.

However poignant and painful your fears are, they are nothing compared to the fear that somehow you have gotten yourself so far away from God that you can't find your way back. There is the terror that you can't reach God because you are not worthy or pure or honest or loving good enough. That is an unconscious, crushing fear, and it's in every one of you. I beg you to look at it.

Please remember, with the fear arises the solution. They are two sides of the same coin. Allow yourself to feel the yearning to be Home, to be at peace, to have love, to be fearless. It is the cry sent from deeply within the soul, and as you move out of the ego-separated motion, you find in the cry itself, in the pain itself, the sweetness of the solution. They arise together. Do not be afraid to allow yourself to be afraid. Allow yourself to acknowledge how far you have traveled in your mind from the experience that *you* are God, alive, dynamic, as you are—pure, conscious awareness.

$\oint \ \oint \ \oint$

What happens if I'm way out there and want to go Home, but I'm afraid "Daddy" is going to be angry?

Are you afraid of my energy field? Has there ever been anything that came to you from it that made you feel unacceptable? You answer, "No." If *this* energy is trustworthy, can you imagine what acceptance awaits you when you are wholly reunited with your Divine Self? The arousal of fear is why I beg you not to listen to anyone who comes to you with a fearful teaching. Whatever credentials they may present, if they spread fear of God, they are not a true mirror of the Divine. So listen to those who tell you that all is well, that you are already always Home. You are Home Itself, Now. Bartholomew, as a metaphor of God-Consciousness, was meant to give you a direct experience of what awaits you. I have told you, God is the greatest Lover in the universe, and He eternally yearns for the return of His beloveds.

The moment you say, "Help me. I, of myself, can do nothing," and mean it, the walk back begins. In truth, everyone who has heard or read these words has begun the journey Home. You are all on your way. Just don't lose the belief that you are on your way. You might even use a little humor and ask to be pushed if necessary. And in the midst of your greatest fear, remember, it is not *the* fear. You do not need to change your life. One little cause does not equal one little effect. I am constantly trying to explode the linear belief that A leads to B, and B to C. You are not a linear experience; you are an explosion of consciousness, and things are always in constant motion. They will change, so just let it happen. You don't have to do anything or change anything in your *outer* world to find God.

Just remember, everything happens to remind you of your deep, inner loneliness. If you think your outer world is a place that needs to be fixed, you will continue to fuss over it all your life. I am not saying that it is not important, and I am not saying that it is not painful. I am simply saying that it is *secondary*. There is pain and there is anguish, but as real as those are, they are not as painful as the fear that you may have done something so offensive to God that your anguish is a punishment for your mistakes.

Whatever you think you are desiring is a camouflage for what you really desire. Start remembering that the camouflage is secondary. That doesn't mean you don't pay attention to your life and work and ask for what you imagine you need. Acknowledge it all, and also that you want to remember what your real purpose is. Because the problem and solution are one, the Light will begin to shine and the power will begin to show Itself. Out of that sweet, quiet calmness, a feeling of gentle continuity will be observed. Pay attention to it because that sense of continuity is the Divine. Move away from the secondary, and place yourself deeply in the primary cry of your life and know that you are already what you are looking for—you are Home Itself.

5

Co-creators of Reality

My friends, between you, you have read almost everything there is to read about awakening to the Self. Yet the inner yearning does not cease. There are times late at night when you feel the pain of it. By day, you try desperately to hold your life together, hoping things will stay in place so a certain amount of harmony and peace can be yours. Then you get upstarts like "me" who tell you that the kinds of peace you are experiencing are very minor in comparison to what is really present. You are told that there is a "mysterious something" underlying life that you have not yet fully experienced. So you again come here on beautiful days like this to allow yourself to break through the barriers of limited consciousness into the limitless.

§ § §

We will simply recreate and restate what you already know. You already have what you need. You already have your own willingness, your own psyche and physical body, your feelings of expectation and your imagination. The only piece missing, the only thing separating you from what you call Enlightenment, is your *belief*, your concept, that you are not the Light of Awareness

Itself. Looking for God was not meant to add to your stress level, but I am afraid that for some of you it has become the greatest stress of all. Finding God was, in fact, meant to be an ongoing feeling, a sense of letting go and allowing that which is always present to bubble up through all of the limiting filters you have placed between you and this state. Instead, it's as if you are playing a game of knowing you are God, then hiding from that reality, and now allowing yourself to come back to it.

It is basically a simple realization we are asking for; that which you seek is present—absolutely, abundantly, totally, and completely present in this moment. It is in this place, within you, outside of you, as far as you can see and beyond. That "mysterious something" is in everything, so there is no other place or time you have to go to and get it. You do not have to shine yourselves up to attract the Light. Purifying yourselves of negative thoughts and becoming more holy will never make you shiny enough because they have nothing to do with finding out you are the Light. Is it not ludicrous to think of the Light having to shine more brightly in order to know itself to be Light? Is it not strange to think you have to become worthy of being what you already are? All you have to do is make a decision.

That decision is, are you willing to believe that you are, at this moment, Enlightenment Itself? There must come a day in your life when you decide. Are you willing to believe two things? One, that God *is;* and two, *you are that, also,* just as you are, without having to change anything about yourself. *Are you willing to accept the truth of what you are and experience that truth moment after moment?*

Your words, your thoughts, and your beliefs have constructed false filters. Although they are only made up of "ideas," they are stronger than steel. Yet, miraculously, those filters can be dissolved in an instant. You begin the dissolving process with one of your most powerful tools, *imagination with intention.*

۶ ۶ ۶

*So we begin. Close your eyes, please, and assume your position of meditation. Please turn your awareness to your breath. Simply allow breathing to be the focus of your awareness. Just gently focus on your breathing. On the in-breath, visualize and **feel** God-Power-Awareness-Consciousness. Whether it means light, energy in motion, the vastness, the void, or something more personal such as Christ or Buddha or a beloved teacher, just feel it as you breathe in. With this visual intention, you are giving your psyche permission to experience the nonphysical. Then on the out-breath, use that power to push past the limits of your body. With the out-breath, make yourselves vaster by feeling and imagining the energy moving out of your body and into space. **That space is filled with what you are looking for.***

*It's as if you gather up and allow yourself to be filled with whatever in your imaginings is the stuff of God-Self; and then, with that expanded breath, you turn it back through the body and out, powerfully, into the space around you. Do this again and again. Allow it, don't force it, but be intent. Feel how vast it is— don't let it be a mental process, **feel** it! The whole purpose of this exercise is to decide that you wish to experience the nonphysical, and then do it! Decide, then do it. Don't stop until you feel the reality of it.*

Pause.

Your senses tell you that you are a "something" inside a body, looking, listening, sensing, tasting, feeling, touching, smelling, and thinking. If you pay attention only to the senses, they will lead you to believe that that is who and what you are. Yet the question is constantly present: "Is *that* all of who I am?" It is the vaster part of you that brings you to ask this question. The vast part of you knows that the answer is "No!" But instead of listening to your own vastness, my friends, you allow your ego-mind to answer the question. You ask, "Is that all?" and the ego-mind says, "No, no, it's not all, but let *me* tell you what more there is."

And in hearing the ego's answer, you become frightened that there may be hidden parts of you that are ugly or weak or unacceptable. If you think that things will always be the same, then you will continue to see what you believe is there. This makes you afraid to truly contemplate the question.

But the tug-of-war goes on. The question continues to be asked, and the ego-mind continues to answer. Then, one day you ask with a different voice, not of the ego, but the voice of your yearning, "Is this physical reality all there is to life?" And then the "teacher" appears. When your being yearns to know, the ego-voice lessens, and the answers begin to come. But the question has to be firmly in place. Do you want to know what is going on in your life? Don't you ever wonder how two people in the same place, subject to the same event, can have two totally different experiences of that event? For one, it is life-changing, and for another, death-producing. So what is going on? *Life* is going on. This is not a closed system or a dead universe. There is something much more miraculous happening each moment. You can be part of that miracle when you really begin to grapple with the questions of Life. So get excited about your ability to remove things from your awareness that you don't want, and to replace them with things that ignite a light in your heart.

§ § §

If you have a deep belief that "this is the way things are, I can't change them," it is the belief that keeps making things remain as they are. Things are changing all the time, and what makes them change into something you want is your willingness to be very clear about *what* you want and your belief that you can have it. *You create what you believe.* I know the world tells you differently, that all of a sudden something outside your control happens to you, and your only part in it is to learn how to respond. But that idea comes from a kindergarten level of consciousness. It won't hold up when you start getting into physics, and it certainly won't explain things when you get to quantum theories. In reality, there is no experience out there that you see clearly and then respond to. In fact, *what you experience is your response to your own belief patterns.* You are not expressing the reality of what you are looking at, but your inner reality of what you believe. *You create what you see by the beliefs you hold about what you are looking at. You do not see them as they really are, but as what your beliefs about them are.*

On one level, thinking you create your own reality can be so depressing that you don't even want to think about it. But keep going. You need to search more deeply, past the fear. If you stop at the belief that your ever-changing thoughts, your ever-vacillating emotions, and your small, vulnerable body create the total vastness of the universe, you have stopped before reaching a real level of truth. Your limited self cannot create the limitless. So don't stop there. You can either dismiss the whole subject by saying something like, "Well, God creates everything," even if you don't really *know* it to be true, or you can begin to be the serious student of the subject of how consciousness creates. The small, ego-based part of you, which you so often take to be all of you, is not capable of creating the vastness, wonder, infinite beauty, and harmony that is the reality of things. How can something disharmonious create harmony? How can something filled with doubt create perfect hope? How can something that thinks life is ugly create beauty? How can something imperfect create perfection?

So you have to deepen your search for the answers. Accept the challenge. The quest is to find out. Who is the creator of this reality? *Take not a blind leap of faith, but a leap of consciousness.* Become gently and *humorously* aware of the emotional, mental, and physical drama that is going on within you. Then acknowledge and *feel* that this accumulation of drama is *not* powerful enough to create the vastness of consciousness. God and you together are creating every moment. So is the small ego. *Which one are you going to be aware of?* The limited ego-self or the god-Self? You are always choosing because you recreate yourself constantly. And in every new moment, you can choose to use the power of peace, love, and joy, or self-pity, judgment, and fear. It's as simple as that. Both are there. Which will you put your conscious power behind?

⸎ ⸎ ⸎

In consciousness, nothing is new, yet everything is new. God is constantly experiencing Itself in endless new ways, yet always containing the ever-present Source of Its unchanging Being. A crystal takes many eons to create. In the depths of the earth, the crystal experiences itself in a certain way. When it goes through the birthing process, being taken up out of the earth, broken away from its source, changed and transformed into different shapes by the alchemy of natural forces or machinery, it begins to experience itself in another way. Now it enters the created world of mankind and is purchased by one of you to be taken home and used for still different purposes. It has been changed by these experiences and has changed the experience of what it touches. This is how a crystal can help heal you. Every event it went through changed it, as it changed those events and people it touched upon; and your journey through life is like that of the crystal, an energy field changing what it touches and being changed in turn.

One dramatic example of this would be the patterns being formed in crop fields all over England in the summertime. At night, something moves onto these fields, making intricate patterns in them, some as long as a football field. No one sees or hears this being done, yet the next day, there they are. Investigators have taken bits of the grass or grain from inside the circles and have subjected them to microscopic inspection. They found that the cellular components, the structural makeup of the grain, had been greatly changed. Where patterns were random before the event, they are now geometrically aligned, often with a center point. They appear like living, beautiful mandalas, with centers and circles radiating outward. Material just a few inches away from the direct impact of the mysterious energy remained the same, but what had been touched was transmuted.

Just as energy touches those fields and changes the shape of grain so that it experiences itself differently, the interaction changes the way the energy experiences itself. *Energies that touch each other change each other.* Something marvelous is happening. Just as England has been a place of spiritual awakening in the past, so is it now. Its fields send out a willingness to have their shapes changed. The result is power, not only to those who look upon it, but also in how the field now experiences itself. Is that too "far out" for you? I hope not, for there are more such events about to take place on this planet.

These events can happen to you as well. Like the ancient fields, you can invite this new energy into you, and the result will be that both you and the energy will experience something new. You and it *together* are experiencing "something new." If you want to create something more alive and exciting, choose the right partner for the job. Will you select the limited self that creates only out of the past, or will you take the risk and dare to call in something vaster? How? State your desire with clarity, feel the desire, hold the expectation of its fulfillment, and be open to results!

When many of you are asked to "Do it now!" or told, "You can do it!" your response often is, "This won't work," How do you reverse such an inner mantra? You are all very intelligent, you are all very creative, and you already know the answer. *You do it by doing it.* How many times have we said this? You become aware of that inner voice that keeps saying, "No, it won't work. It's never worked, and it never will work." You listen until you hear clearly whatever doubts the voice is presenting; and with sweet, gentle firmness, you say a full, abundant *no* to it. We are going to do a simple experiment that I feel will show you that this can be done.

§ § §

Please take a few deep breaths and become aware of how your body feels at this moment. Take time and feel your breath. Buried within your awareness is one particularly painful view of yourself that cripples your ability to enjoy your life and yourself. Identify just what that is. Name it with either a word, a phrase, a belief, or make it a visual remembrance. See it clearly. Be very specific. It could be something physical, mental, or emotional, some way of seeing yourself that you cannot reconcile and allow in your life, something you constantly fight against. Just gently identify it.

Pause.

*Now, having identified it, I want you to spend a little while repeating this phrase: "I am . . ." whatever this "negative" is. Repeat the same thing, again and again. Please put all of the power of your awareness on this. And I want you to pay attention to **how your body feels as you are saying this about yourself.** This is important. Repeat the phrase to yourself for **no longer than two minutes.** Use a timer if necessary.*

Pause.

*Now, ask yourself what energy could come and move through you that would change the **feeling** that the previous statement left in your body. What energy can you imagine that would dilute and dissolve that feeling? It may not necessarily be the **opposite** of the feeling, but another energy that could come in and make the change. Be very specific. Is it Peace? Love? Acceptance?*

Laughter? Forgiveness? Let this new energy field flow over the original feeling. Repeat it with your mind, feel the feeling in you, and allow it to flood the old feeling with the fullness of the "new." And feel the newness.

Do this for as long as you can. Use music if possible. Visualize that vortex of energy in any way that seems appropriate to you. See it moving through and carving new shapes in you. That's all you need to dwell on. It moves through you, carving new shapes. The energy you have chosen is impressing you as it impressed the fields. Make this as real as you possibly can. Together you create a "new you," a new feeling, a new belief.

End of exercise.

§ § §

You have no idea how sacred every moment of your life is. You think that only the moments when you are doing holy things are sacred. This is false. Every instant God is creating with you, *changing Itself and you* as well. Science has discovered that 300 million cells in your body die every minute. That's a lot of change! Your ego is not aware of this process, so "who" is doing this? It is the real "I" of your Being, which is the I of God in Its vastness, participating in this process. You are constantly being sculpted, reshaped, and reformed by the Divine, and this is what makes every moment sacred. God is new every moment. God is not boring, God is not bored. God is in a state of delight about being God-in-action and about this sculpting and changing process. Any change is exciting, because it is all God-in-action, experiencing Itself ever new from moment to moment.

The small you is the one stuck with experiencing yourself the same way, over and over. You go down the same street to work and see the same houses. There is constant repetition. So it is with your consciousness. You go down the same paths of consciousness over and over, and in the end you are bored. I am asking you to be *excited* by the possibility of change. You change with the help of a deep desire and willingness to respond to your life in a different way. If you don't want to feel or react in a certain manner, be aware of that. *Do not automatically move to the opposite.* Please do not polarize yourself by thinking the opposite of what you are trying to change is the only answer. Many energy fields are eternally present for you to choose from. Fear may be changed by love, anger by humor, sorrow by gratitude. Do not let your intellect be the only part of your psyche to give you the answer.

Each part of the process is essential. You must *know* something is happening that you wish to change; you must *yearn* to have one of those eternal powers move in and change the field of your consciousness, and you must *allow* it to do so. Most important, *you must have patience.* In this day of the quick fix, if the change doesn't come about quickly, you try something else, and if it still doesn't work, you forget it. But this kind of creative resculpting is a moment-to-moment process that takes patience and practice.

$ $ $

You are surrounded with all kinds of experiential data to support your hope that God-Awareness is real, so watch for it and assimilate it. It will vitalize your hopes and add energy to your yearnings! Instead of paying attention to the gloom-and-doom data that is also available, decide to be responsible for *choosing* which reality you want to be a part of. If you were a schoolteacher with the conscious intention of using those school hours to amass God-filled data for yourself, you would begin to see it, feel it, and experience it all during the school day. You would find yourself dwelling on the goodness, beauty, wonder, spontaneity, and harmony that is in the students, in yourself, and in your surroundings. However you "see" a child is often what is reflected back to you. So at the end of your day, you will either be excited or exhausted.

Many of you often walk into your personal "classrooms" with no intention of amassing new data. You are there to validate and expand on the data you already have. If you are not willing to create a new way of seeing, today is going to look exactly like yesterday. But if you hold the intention and willingness to create things a little differently, the old will drop away, and things will move with a little more freedom and spontaneity. No one need be stuck in the past. As you are ready to see something new, *something new comes.* So if you don't like your life, your emotions, or your thoughts, you can carve out something much more harmonious for yourself and others.

The desire for change is very much alive in the world. Many people yearn to see a new, enlightened, balanced planet. But to make this a reality means that *you are going to have to change the shape of your own awareness.* These changes can only come to the Earth plane through human awareness. You must make the necessary inner changes. Changing the shape of one feeling, such as anger, will help create a less angry world. The key to transformation is the willingness to change those inner shapes. The difficult part, as you will find, is making the decision that you really *do* want to change.

You came to this planet *to become aware that God is your True Nature.* It is the most holy thing you could possibly do here and the most joyful.

6

Choices

I am quite sure the minds and hearts of most of you today are focused on what is happening in the area you call the Middle East.[1] I would like to start out making a basic statement about these events, and then go into them in depth. The basic statement is essential. This event is not some kind of mistake. This war did not just happen when God's back was turned, and things now have to be made right. This conflict is part of the way the energy moves on this planet at this time. Please hold on to the truth that this very important event ultimately has to do with the expansion of consciousness. It is here to teach all of you, and the meaning of these events must be resolved deeply within yourself on a personal basis.

⚜ ⚜ ⚜

What is happening now is important, and every important event on this planet has ultimately to do with the expansion of *world* consciousness, global consciousness. Global consciousness is the ability of all of you to make deep changes in the way you

---

[1] In January of 1991, the United States found itself once again at war. Tensions in the Middle East had caused an explosion in Iraq that would involve many nations in a violent conflict that was to last less than two months. — Editor

work with such events. You are part of this process! It is not separate from you, nor is it separate from all those watching it. Through television, this event will be played out globally, meaning it will be watched by most conscious people on the planet. It will be played on a world stage. And everyone who participates through even viewing this confrontation will be a part of it, consciously or unconsciously. Remember, God uses *everything* to bring you Home, so let us describe how you can consciously use this.

You, personally, can either make this moment expansive for the planet as a whole, or a missed opportunity. You all have different ways of looking at the world, with different areas within your body perceiving things differently, one from the other. You are aware of your physical eyes and what you see with them. You are also aware of how you "see" with your mind, which we will refer to as seeing with your "mental eye." You have an inner vision that has been called the "spiritual eye." And when you see with this spiritual eye, your vision is full of Light. How does this apply to what we are talking about?

As you sit in front of the television, you "see" what is happening. Your first level of response is going to be mixed. A part of you may be very angry, and other parts may feel righteous, sad, afraid, or as violent as anything you are seeing "out there." You can help by being aware of all these responses. This is not the place to say, "No, no, I am a spiritual being and this has nothing to do with me. I am above all this." Move away from that position, and get deeply into the visceral, cellular responses, even though they may be very upsetting to you. It is not easy to admit that there is violence within you. When you see this, *don't try to talk yourself out of it.* That will not work in the long run.

Make a clear statement of your response. "When I see what is happening out there, I become angry! I become afraid," or "I have visions of the revenge I would like to see effected on those people." Pay attention to *whatever* your response is. Don't deny it in any way; just become aware of what it is in as nonjudgmental a manner as possible. This is the way the physical eye sees things. So let's just for the moment call it your *observed response.*

The second way of seeing things is with what we are calling the mental eye. That vision includes the world of ideas, beliefs, projection—your "mental world." When you talk about this war to people you thought you knew rather well, you may experience a mental surprise. You all have different points of view! Your point of view is the point from which events are seen by you. It is a point of reference in your mind, arrived at from the accumulation of every single thought, every single word you've read, and everything you've been told. As you view things from your mental perspective, you start to run into other people's different points of view. People you thought you communicated with, mind to mind, turn out to be coming from another level entirely, with the result that you feel that no joining between you is possible.

If you get stuck trying to force your point of view about what is going on and what your country should do about it onto others, you will end up with a lot of mental headaches and seriously disturb some very nice relationships. This is not the level where you have to be in alignment with someone else, and it is certainly not the level where deep healing and joining take place. So please understand this, and give everyone in your life the freedom to see what they see and think what they think. You can have very different beliefs about this war and still be joined in care and friendship.

Let us say that you were brought up in a military family. If so, you will take a very definite position about this conflict. If you were raised in a family that has been in the peace movement for a long time, or if you have lived in ashrams or as a renunciant, you are going to have ideas that are very, very different. And if you are asking me who is right, my response is still the same. We cannot go to the mental world and decide "who is right"! We can only say, you are who you are. To say one person is right and one is wrong would mean judging you on the level of your learned responses. It is very unfair to judge others on things that they have no control over. There would then be something "wrong" with one of you. And if something is wrong, you will need to be "fixed." And the "fixing" goes on endlessly.

Instead of judging, become aware that you have mental "eyes," and then look carefully at your mental view of the world, of life, of what is. When you speak, be aware of what you are saying! Listen closely to yourself raising whatever flag you are in favor of, trying to convince others that yours is the "right" one. Be who you are, say what you think, and do as you do, but please listen to yourself. Listen and ask yourselves what *deep beliefs* stand behind your ideas.

As you talk to other people, often you are not paying attention to these deep belief structures. Listen and ask yourself, "How did I get that particular idea? Who told me this is the way it should be?" Bring the belief closer and inspect it so you can begin to understand how these thoughts arose and how they became yours. Then, with kindness and compassion, you may be able to realize that whoever it is you are talking to comes from their own set of beliefs over which they have no control. And it's all right! No attack is necessary! This realization will create an inner space that you can relax into. You are all very tense, and, in your words, "uptight;" or even more, "uptight and squeaking"! It's a phrase that works well here. Do you all recognize that tight, painful place within you? It's like you've run your car without enough lubricant and it begins to make a certain sound. That happens in you, also. When you begin to squeak inside, please realize that there is *something more at stake here than you thought.* And that "something more" is very, very important.

That "something more" is a frightened voice inside you telling you, *"This is the way the world is. Things will never change!"* Some of you feel, "This is the way the world is. There will always be fighting. It's man's nature to fight," while others feel, "This is the way the world is. Peace is the basic component of all consciousness, and war must be eliminated." Your view might fall between the two, but instead of trying to change *their* mind, know your own. Keep remembering that this situation is here, once again, to mirror your beliefs and ideas back *to you.* And please, my friends, I beg you not to badger each other on this belief level. Do not take up weapons, verbal or otherwise, because if you do, I tell you frankly that you are not helping. If on this mental level you try to change, convince, cajole, and manipulate, you are not helping to awaken any manifestation of a global consciousness.

Your job, if you want to help this situation, is to be totally aware of your physical and mental "eyes," while remaining very strongly conscious that you have *another* set. You have what is called the *spiritual eye.* The *third eye of consciousness,* that *real* entrance to the other levels of awareness, opens when you begin to ask, "How can I help? How can I bring a sense of peace to this chaos, my own chaos as well as the world's?" Close the other eyes, and you will "see" with a perception past all the physical and mental planes of separation. The spiritual eye allows you to see where the true point of centering is.

Many of you are afraid to reach that center over this issue, because you are afraid if you come to peace within yourself, you somehow are not going to be helping your country in this war effort. Please do not respond to this statement now; just think about it for a while. It is important. Let us say you have a child, a loved one, or a friend in the Gulf. You want to do something to support them, and there is a part of you that feels that if you are seated in a place of peace over all this, you are not helping those you care about; you are letting them down. Beloved friends, I want to respond to this as deeply as I can and say that the greatest help any one of you can give is this: As many moments as possible, get to that centered place inside you; breathe peace into it as best you can while holding the entire situation in your mind, and allow those moments of peace to move clearly and deeply into and over that situation. Breathe quietness and balance into your felt sense of the whole complicated issue. Breathe and breathe, and your heart will expand.

It is your peace of heart that is going to help! Do not deny or run away from any chaotic motion, but keep holding to that steady inner center. Feel it fully. You are a human being, and you have been trained as a human being. Part of that, for many of you, is to believe in and fight for your country, whatever country happens to be "yours" this time. *You don't need to get rid of that belief!* But you can move from a deep point of inner power and bathe the entire situation with the "third eye" of steady love and wisdom. The rest of your responses, who is right and who is wrong, may be human and normal, but giving in or adding to them is going to help the situation very little. There is not one of you who cannot find that place of peace within, even if it's only for a few moments at a time. The more you practice, the more you will find yourself familiar with this quiet place within you, and the more you will be able to use it in *whatever* difficulty you might find yourself.

This eruption of violence in the Middle East, or any violent outbreak, natural or otherwise, is an important event for consciousness, and it can be used. The way most humans learn, and the way consciousness expands on the Earth plane, is through observation. With television and modern methods of communicating visual and verbal material, the entire population of the planet will see what war *really* is, if governments allow honesty in the sharing of what is really happening. It will not be a distant, idealized conflict, but an immediate, personal observation that will reveal the basic nature of war.

$ $ $

Your country finished another war not too long ago. There is an idea that the fighting in Vietnam was some "dirty" kind of war, and there are deep hopes that this one will be different. There is no question this will be very, very different! Why? Because of the lessons deeply learned by the human psyche *as a result of the war in Vietnam.* Every one of you who had access, either through participating, reading, seeing, or hearing what went on at that time, affected those events, and was affected by them.

It was those few who went to that country and fought there who brought back the awareness of war and what it really means. It started with them, with what they did, what they suffered, and what they learned. There are many ways to be a hero, and one way is to return from a war with the knowledge of *"This* is the way war really is, and this is not what I choose to do again." Now, as you move into another conflict, you come to it with the knowledge that all those heroes gained. That knowledge is now part of your beliefs about war.

Is this conflict something you want for your planet? This is a very important question, and your answer is even more important. The war is not just something that is taking place "over there." As you respond to it by watching the television or listening to the radio or reading the newspaper, you are affecting the situation with your response day by day. *Day by day you make a difference!* There is no separation in human consciousness. You are *not* separate from Saddam Hussein. You are *not* separate from the ability to influence him in whatever way you choose, if this is your desire. *He* is not a closed circuit. He is open, just as you all are. I am asking you to take the highest stance you know and come from that level. If you do, there is a *possibility* this kind of intensity sent out, not only to him but to his entire country, will begin to bring about an awakening. Let us not just have this be a victory of arms. Let this be a victory of consciousness, so when it is finished, there will be a level of awareness set in the land and in the people that will, in some future moment, begin to open to a deeper understanding of what is now considered to be the enemy.

As world opinion begins to amass itself, the psychic pressure on that country is going to grow. What Iraq will do as a result of it is not yet determined. You can help make this event something that expands consciousness if you will be open to the entire situation. I am asking you to live with *full* awareness. As you lose awareness and slip back down into your automatic mental ideas and physical responses, you will not be helping as much as you could. So take being part of a world event as your destiny, and choose to make a difference with your conscious awareness. Mankind needs One Consciousness—alive, dynamic, expansive, and above all, loving—and this is the way to begin. I know for some of you that this is displeasing. I totally understand. Do exactly what you need to do. You are who you are, and you respond the way you need to, but please, my friends, *to whatever extent you can,* be aware of what you are doing. *Your thoughts matter. Your energy matters.*

§ § §

You are all excited about the changes you hope will be in place by the year 2000. What happens in the Middle East plays an important part in these changes. Instead of looking at the small view, let us pull back and expand it. If this is not some kind of global mistake that happened when God wasn't watching, but indeed a series of events that is important for the wholeness of things, we have to get as long a view of it as we can. Remember God! Please do not get so small with this situation that you forget the Divine. Those of you who are not meditating, will you find five minutes a day, just *five minutes* a day, to focus on peace and visualize it on this planet? Those of you who are good at it, do it more. And those of you who are beginning, please try harder. Visualize this planet absolutely radiant, bathed totally in Light, Power, Love, and Harmony. When you do this, you are moving away from limited beliefs into expanded possibilities.

Some of you are ready to move out of a limited idea of global consciousness into something bigger. Obviously, you move away from a limited belief structure by creating and moving into something vaster. This is magnificently exciting, and yet it can be very difficult because you have one foot rooted in the past, "my country right or wrong," and the other is poised to step into a future world with the hope of one planet, one people. You are creating a whole new world view, and you have to work at it. You don't build a successful company by thinking about your vacations! You build your company by thinking about what you can do to make it successful. So it is with this. You have to work at it.

You know that *energy follows thought.* It's going to begin through people who want to make the thought-form reality, not just a "nice idea." You start on the mental plane with the idea, "Wouldn't it be magnificent to have a planet filled with excitement, peace, and harmony?" Then with the wisdom and power of the third eye, you hold the idea as a vision. That becomes a feeling tone within you, and as you visualize that for the planet, you move the energy of thought through the mental, down to the physical level. As you begin to build the power of it by holding to your vision day after day, you will start to feel the energy in your body. This grounds it in the physical, and in the process, you will be uplifted.

I say this again and again: *Work for God.* He always pays His bills! What do I mean? When you work toward global peace, global love, and global harmony, *which is the absolute destiny of this planet, you are doing God's will.* Your payoff will be the harmony and expansion *you* will feel as you move your body, mind, and emotions into alignment. That which you are hoping and praying for, for the world, is what you will begin to receive for yourself. The gifts of God are right here in the kind of action we are asking from you. As you give to others, so you receive. It is the law. As you hold this planet in your heart with love and harmony and the wonderful excitement of humankind aligned, you will become that which you are giving.

God never asks you to do *anything* that does not increase the love in your heart, the harmony in your awareness, and the compassion of your being. What we are asking for today is something very specific. What you give in these next few weeks and months you will also receive—deeply. We need you. We need your help, as you need ours. We are all in this together—one mind, one heart.

When you work toward global peace, global love, and global harmony, which is the absolute destiny of this planet, you are doing God's will.

7
Planetary Purpose

ALBUQUERQUE, NEW MEXICO

Last month we pointed out that whatever beliefs you have about what is happening in the Middle East are going to be your own. They will differ according to who you are, the country you live in, and your own personal background. I would like to present a point of view in which to fit these differences. Historically, the consciousness of this planet has unfolded in isolated groups. Asian cultures, for example, differ greatly from those of the United States. Until recently, you were not very aware of each other and had little real, individual global communication. All that is changing. Planetary consciousness is moving from the isolation of separated countries toward an interconnectedness, through countries sharing with, and caring for, each other.

§ § §

The purpose of this planet is to Love. If you wish to understand how this works, take your ideas about war, particularly this war, and look at it from the point of view of planetary Love. I know this is difficult, but you must understand: God's delight is the extension of Love into ever-greater areas of consciousness.

There has been a slow but steady expansion in the hearts and minds of mankind as you moved out to cover the globe and learned to love greater numbers of people. You found love came when agreement between you was present. Your sense of loving and being loved was lost when too much disagreement arose. So what is needed is a way to increase your areas of agreement and decrease those of disagreement.

The more people you can agree with and feel at ease and relaxed around, the more the tension between you dissipates. Those boundaries of separation soften and become more gentle. If you are missing love in your life, you may be looking at the differences rather than the similarities between you and other people. As you relax and soften around the seeming separations, you will be participating in the expansion of planetary love. The greater the love in the world, the greater the potential for future love. It moves out in ever-expanding waves.

When the people of different cultures in the Middle East begin to interact within their countries, they carry the potential for mutual understanding. Each time they talk to one another, the possibility is there. When there is an attempt at understanding, then agreement is possible and love can arise! For a long time, the Middle East has represented to you, and you to them, two closed systems, two foreign bodies that seemed inscrutable and mysterious. Since they are not alike, there is always a tendency for each to feel that *their* system is superior. Feelings of superiority make love almost impossible. There is very little understanding or communication between these systems; therefore, they contain no wisdom of the heart. Hearts can be moved under extremities such as war because both sides share the same basic fears and confusion. Therein lies the *opportunity* for love. There is a chance to drop the mental beliefs and respond to one another through the understanding of the heart, knowing another individual is facing the same fears you are. Such a recognition of similarities brings hope of an ending to hatred and conflict.

It is only when physical bodies get together that understanding has a chance. I mean that literally, because the faculty of understanding the other person's point of view is not in the mind. You may agree with many different points of view in theory, but in actual fact, theories cannot make you feel love or create a space for an inner knowing of the *similarities* between you. When this war is finished, something very interesting will begin happening. Some Americans and other allies will be left to live in the Middle East, where they can begin to gain a new understanding of their surroundings based on similarities. They, in turn, will be able to influence those others who now stand so far apart. Being exposed to the influence of these countries can help them break out of the limited boundaries. What is necessary to take advantage of this opportunity is the willingness to acknowledge the presence of a different point of view, and to see how that does not necessarily make others separate, just *interesting*.

Frankly, war is not the maximum way to bring about this kind of understanding. *I am by no means raising the flag of war,* saying that God wants it so you can all have a chance to love. But I want to repeat something I have said from the first year we met: God uses *everything* to bring you Home. *Anything you create,* God can use to reveal a quality of love that can unite this planet in a knowledge of Oneness. That is the point of this God experiment. How you come to this is your choice. I want you to deeply understand the beauty of this. It means no matter how diabolical, dark, or painful your life may be, the same basic law applies. No matter what drama and war are going on in your thoughts, feelings, or actions, each moment can be used by the Divine within. You need to be willing to have it happen. Just ask!

§ § §

I would like to remind you again that many of you have identified yourselves with what you call your ego, what I call your "small self." Your small self does not contain the eternality of truth within it. The ego is simply a conglomerate or cluster of different beliefs you hold. These beliefs are constantly changing. If you find one piece of information you didn't previously have, a long-held belief you would have died for just evaporates, and you have a totally different point of view. Your ego does not have the eternality of Truth, just of change.

You believe one thing one moment, yet the opposite under different circumstances. You will find when you begin to watch your belief structures that many of these beliefs do not agree with each other *at all*. You say things such as, "War is evil," yet you also say, "Our way must prevail because we are right." You show an inconsistency in *many* of your beliefs. Are you clear about what you are defending in the middle of a desert on the other side of the world? Please stop a moment and ask yourself what these beliefs are and how much you need to defend them.

There is no solid center point within the ego to give it consistent direction. The ego is *exactly* like clouds in the sky. You defend to the death your love affairs, your children, your individual rights, your jobs—all of it! Yet your beliefs about these situations are constantly changing. You are defending clouds that shift about and dissipate endlessly, not only from moment to moment and year to year, but from lifetime to lifetime. You "come in with" some of your beliefs, and you have never stopped to examine them and see if you still wish to maintain them or stop focusing on them.

The ego is not a very useful place to go to in order to look at the larger picture of your life. There is no unifying nucleus in it that tells you which would be the best way for you to move. It does not consistently say, "God is over here," or "Goodness is over there," or even, "This will make me happy." With nothing to direct it, going first in one direction, then another, the ego keeps you in motion all the time. You call that motion "living." Your beliefs all exist within the ego-structure. Some come and bump up against you and leave, while others just float in very quietly and stay with you, day after day. It is helpful to understand the very fragile, unpredictable, and inconsistent nature of ego motion. When you stop looking for a central, continuous, ongoing "you" in that structure, you will begin to experience an "I" that is more vast. You experience a state of vast, benevolent equilibrium. Within that vastness, the ego and its manifestations simply move here and there. They come and go by themselves, always flowing into and out of the moment. These thoughts are not going anywhere in particular, nor are they moving toward any "grand purpose." They simply come and go.

Where, then, do you go to get the focus that you want for your peace of mind and heart? How do you place your feet firmly on the road to God? Let us go back to the analogy of the sky and the clouds. The clouds are present; and the empty, vast Sky is the Divine mind of consciousness, that pure, conscious awareness you have come to call God. It is that unlimited immensity that silently and majestically allows all of the comings and going of the clouds. There can be the greatest thunderstorm imaginable, and the sky is not affected. You could not even see the clouds if it were not for the illumination from the sky. This is the Light of God-Consciousness that is contained within the magnificent wholeness of the vast, ever-present sky. Magically, the Light is within the light. Consciousness *is* luminescent Light, and it doesn't need another power source to provide that illumination. It comes from within Itself.

It would help to stop a moment and identify with the vastness of Sky. You can visualize it deeply out of your own consciousness, holding the image so it becomes more familiar and can fill an expanded place in your psyche. As you imagine this, do you not begin to feel something else present? Do you get any sense of a vaster feeling for yourself? The ego will say, "You're making that up. It's just your imagination. Forget it. The reality is the clouds." Do not believe the ego! Keep identifying with the vast Sky.

When you really begin to pay attention to the ever-changing flux of your thoughts and beliefs, you will become aware that, although there is thinking, *there is no thinker.* Have you ever really found a thinker inside yourself? You have a brain, but what motivates it? Where do ideas come from? How do beliefs arise? What's really going on? As you begin to ponder these questions, many of you will realize that, in your pursuit of God-Consciousness, you are trying to find a *person,* a thinker or a doer inside you. But *is* there one?

For those of you who are ready for a new kind of awareness in these troubled times, we ask you to allow yourself to feel the possibility that there is no thinker, no doer. Allow yourself to entertain the chance that you are a very loose conglomerate of belief structures you "think" are acting in unison. Confusion arises because of your identification with your body and your thoughts. Since they are so obviously present, you have come to believe that this body and mind is "you." Well, is it? If that is true, when the body dies, where is the "you" that was so identified with that structure? I know I am asking for a lot of expansion this morning, and some of you may decide that it is too big a stretch, but I am trying, in the time we have left, to bring this truth to its finest focus. There will be a wonderful moment of delight when you realize that that which you have identified as "you" is nothing more than an ever-shifting, ever-changing conglomerate of beliefs. There are other beliefs that will bring you much more peace and joy. *Is your present awareness of Who You Are the one you want to have for the rest of this life?* Please take a few moments to really answer this question.

It is misidentification that is causing the confusion. When you say, "There is *somebody* here," you identify that somebody as the nucleus of a belief structure called ego. I am trying to tell you that is *not* the definition. That is *not* the truth. That *is not* truth. What you are is that which is asking the question of who you are, who is aware of "something very subtle," which is this mysterious, unnameable, yet totally knowable consciousness. It is ever-present, ever-present, *ever-present!* It is *always there,* and *that* is the Awareness asking the question of Itself. It has *nothing* to do with the ever-changing manifestation of what you would call your limited ego-self.

৳ ৳ ৳

People often come to me saying they are on the spiritual path, which means that they work hard in their inner world and do everything they think will help move them toward their goal of God-Consciousness. The individual approaches may vary, but each person is doing their best. They read spiritual material— they meditate, they pray, and they still feel they are not getting anywhere and are unable to move those things they wish to leave behind. We often discover together that these people are taking their learning experiences and teachings, and placing them as *ideas* in their ego structures. For example, you read a book that says, "The Light of God is alive within your heart now." You put that book down. "Right! The Light of God is alive within my heart now!" Finished. You want to know this, you *think* you know it, but nothing has changed. You have been given one of the vastest truths possible, which you take only as an idea and stick into your ego conglomerate. Having explained it away, the ego would have you *forget about it* and you never take the next step! The next step is to *make that truth yours,* putting your awareness there moment after moment, day after day, year after year. Just the *hearing* of truth does not set you free. You must make it your own by keeping it constantly in your awareness.

God is always inspiring you through the written word, through speech with each other, through ideas and dreams, through fear and sorrow, as well as hope and joy. God inspires you in all ways. When you feel that inspiration, it is a knowing in your physical body that you and the Source of that inspiration are joined. People sometimes ask me if *A Course in Miracles*[2] is "real" or not. *A Course in Miracles* inspires whom it inspires, and does so beautifully. Other people read the same book, and nothing happens. Does this mean that there is something faulty with the book or with the person reading it? Not at all! Each of you is inspired in your own ways, and your main responsibility is to move from the point of seeker to the point of finder by *acknowledging those things that make you light up!*

If it is only one sentence, take it and run it through your awareness as often as you can. Put it into the vast sky of your Being, rather than the cloud structures of your ego. If you practice this, things begin to relax in and around you; and the vast, empty sky then empowers you directly through whatever information it was that excited you. As you move the information through your consciousness, you make it your own experience. Then when you speak it, you will be very, very clear about its meaning. You will be speaking from experience, with a power that moves out and makes whatever *you* say true. It is your consciousness moving through your physical body that goes out into the world to ultimately change this planet.

Many of you wish to be "called by God." In truth, my friends, *God is calling you all the time.* How do you *receive* that call? *How does God inspire you in your life?* Ask yourself that question in the weeks ahead. What things bring you closer to the inspiration of Divine Consciousness? As you look at your life, many of you will find that a lot of it is not inspiring. Even some of the highest teachings can become *very* boring because they do not excite you. So look at your life. If there is anything in it that is a *real obstacle* to your finding the God within you, identify it clearly, acknowledge it, and ask yourself, *"What would I have in its place?"* Seated quietly in your home, you can begin this process that will change your life by allowing yourself to dare to create new beliefs from the things you yearn for. *Your yearnings are the*

---

[2] A Course in Miracles, *Foundation for Inner Peace, 1977.*

beginning of your future. Your yearnings now are what end up as reality down the line. Whatever you have in your life is there because some part of you wanted it there, at some time, for some reason. The power and focus to deeply get what you want does not come from the ego-consciousness. So we are back where we started. The yearning is not in the cluster of clouds; it is in the sky!

The clouds are your desires. There is a lot of difference between *desire* and *yearning*. A desire can change in any moment, or from moment to moment. Desires are like wanting tea one day and coffee the next. Yearnings rise up out of the deepest part of you. You may escape to the ends of the universe, but you can't get away, because you take the yearning with you. *Acknowledge it!* That yearning is the voice of the Divine trying to move you to a more open position. Left to itself, consciousness always moves toward greater and greater bliss, greater and greater love, greater and greater understanding. These are the deep things you yearn for. How else can God find you? It is through those yearnings that you keep transcending all of the limitations, doubts, and negative things your reality says to you. You are not responsible for figuring out *how* your yearnings will be fulfilled. You are responsible for allowing yourself to get very, very big with this feeling; and to have a great, deep intimacy with your yearnings.

Intimacy is something you have with yourself. Because there are no boundaries, out of that intimacy with yourself, you can feel intimate in the presence of others. Being intimate with yourself means you know yourself so well that you know you *are* your yearnings. They are part of the sky, and you are part of the sky. The yearning for God-Consciousness comes from the soul, from the depths of your Being. It defines who you are. Find out what you yearn for, and you will know this. It can be frightening when a deep yearning surfaces. You may be afraid to follow your yearnings. You may be afraid that your life will be a disaster. God never said It didn't have the ability to explode things in order to move you on. If it is time to move on to something else, the explosion will happen; and it is best that you be aware, and feel the joy of it, as you fly through the air!

Take your *mind* off your yearnings, because the mind will throw you back into that ever-changing ego structure. Just feel the *potential* inherent in them. They bring new life. Be as honest with yourself as you can, and live out of the true center of your Being. The desires of the ego are capricious, and rise and fall as fast as your breath. But those yearnings for peace, love, harmony, beauty, compassion, understanding, humor, and wisdom that come from the groundswell of your Being, which is the God-Self, reflect with luminescent wonder the sky of consciousness. They will continue to do so until that yearning finds the way to make it happen. It may take one moment a day, one step at a time, but trust your yearnings. Live with them. Make them vast; make them real. Give them the power of your awareness. "Knock and it will open." If yearning is present, seeing Who You Are is very near, and a way *will* open.

I ask you to be at peace in your hearts over all that is going on. Please remember, from the "God side" of things, the love of mankind is moving out across the globe; and if the first steps toward global unity are taken through war, they will not be the last. There will be softer, gentler footsteps that follow. There is *nothing* created by human consciousness that the power of the Divine cannot use for Its own end. And there is but one end—*total Love, manifesting in each of you, for each of you on this planet.* Nothing short of that is going to suffice. That is the goal, and it is a worthy one. You must understand the importance of what is happening, and hold in your heart and mind the view from a higher watch. The more you do, the sooner the ending time of the chaos. If you want to help stop fear, pain, and war, just know that your and everyone else's basic nature is Love, that the unconditional love is always there, closer than your breath. Find every way you can to move into love, whatever that means to you, my friends. This planet will be an incredible constellation of power in the universe when it is radiating nothing but conscious love. Do you sense its destiny and your part in it? You picked it and were wise to do so. I suggest you get on with it.

*Is your present
awareness the
understanding
you want to
have for eternity?*

PART IV

Return

8

The Wave and the Void

This morning I would like to restate, look again at, and go back to some basic concepts of consciousness. I am assuming that you are feeling very bored and dissatisfied with your limited model of who you are and what you are able to experience, and are looking for an explosion of expansive consciousness. In order to help you along, I would like to spend some time talking about the difference between pure, conscious awareness and pure awareness. They are both interesting and vast concepts.

ৠ ৠ ৠ

In the early days of our sharing, I attempted to describe what the ever-present energy looks like. Envision a multicolored wave that has a marvelous sound to it. The colors are translucent and intense; and the sounds are deep and alive, beyond anything you can imagine. This marvelous, magnificent wave of energy is filled with billions of points of light.

Now this wave is moving through something. That "something" is pure awareness. Pure awareness is *not* the wave. Pure, *conscious* awareness is the wave. What's the difference? Pure awareness has no form to it. It is the void. It is called the void because it has no shape and no form. It is called Emptiness because it *has* no shape or form, and it is called the Silence because it has no sound.

In the midst of the void is a magnificent, vast wave that you are a part of, extending out into and being upheld by the formless void. I do not wish to label this void God; because many people have formed their own idea of what God looks like, sounds like, and feels like. That God is not formless; it is a personification of the formless. That personified reality is what you would call your High Self, an intimate place where you go for your safety, your protection, and your sense of being connected to some form that can comfort and understand you. When we refer to anything that has form, we are talking about pure, conscious awareness. A personified God has a form, and our wave of energy is a form, so in both cases we identify them as pure, conscious awareness.

Pure awareness, on the other hand, is that place where all is in total, perfect balance, and therefore at perfect rest. It is the place containing the *totality* of potentiality, meaning that resting within this still "some thing" is *all* the potentiality of consciousness. In some beginning, when this potentiality wanted to experience motion, color, sound, differences, extending, imploding, and so on, consciousness came about. Out of pure awareness came an *explosion* of power, the delightful wave of consciousness you have been riding ever since.

$$\textit{\j} \textit{\j} \textit{\j}$$

My friends, this is no small journey you are on. Just as that explosion created different ways to be aware of itself, so then does each separate part of that consciousness now have the ability to create its own potentiality, its own life, its own reality, and its own sense of "who it is." I think you sometimes forget the amazing delight and wonder of this process. Each creation is as important as any other. The life you are living, no matter how it appears to you, is as important, exciting, and expansive as any life of any other one of the created.

My job is to break up the crystallized, linear ideas you have of who you are and what you are able to experience. Because you, as limited consciousness, have chosen to play in a time/space continuum of your own making, you have also chosen to forget the spontaneous knowledge that every moment the vast awareness is creating everything that comes into the moment. Another way of saying it is: *You, as awareness, create each other every time you look at each other.* Is that not an exciting statement? You create the person, your response to them, and you very much create their response to you. You have lost the excitement that goes with that moment-to-moment creation, because you are locked into patterns of repetition, believing that you are limited and cannot create another "point of view." Consciously or unconsciously, you are locked into the memory of events that happened in the past, and you have forgotten you can leave them behind anytime you want.

You are experiencing yourself as one of the tiny particles floating in the energy wave. In our remaining time together, I want you to learn the skill of taking the focus of your awareness out of that small, limited viewpoint of that tiny particle, and placing it in other areas of consciousness so you can experience something other than "yourself." This is why prayer, meditation, and introspection can all work. Do any of them long enough and you lose awareness of that small self and simply become the action happening. You have consciously taken your awareness off the small self and consciously placed it in a vaster arena of awareness, thereby experiencing what is in it and a vaster part of "who you are."

All areas of consciousness, up to the pure awareness of the very silent heart of potentiality, are available to you now. There are no limits unless you choose to manufacture them. It doesn't matter how many limits you create as long as you *know* you can withdraw your awareness from them at any time, place it in something larger, and then begin to experience that vaster Self. At night, when you are in the desert or the mountains or on the sea, as you look up at the stars, you often feel yourself a part of it all. Suddenly, you are no longer self-absorbed; you are absorbed in a large awareness of Being, into a larger energy field.

This may happen "in spite of you." You don't know how, but you want to experience this shift at will. In our last two sessions together, we practiced expansion. We practiced stretching your awareness to the walls and past them. The minute you find you can do it even in a small way, you will become excited about being able to do it in a vast way! So you must relax into this basic quality of consciousness. Take your awareness and remove it from any point it happens to be focused on, and focus it on a vaster space. Keep on practicing until it becomes almost automatic. When thought is not necessary, stop focusing on thoughts and focus on the vastness.

§ § §

When does the artist enjoy art? When there is no artist present as the art is happening. Creation is taking place, but there is no thinking about every stroke or color used. The artist is occupying a vaster space in that moment. The greater the artist's capacity to fall into this other space, the greater the work. You can say what you want about van Gogh, but I want to tell you, he was not mad. Confused, yes. Reentry from painting experiences such as *Starry Night* was difficult for him because he had a basic belief that life on the Earth plane was painful and financially frustrating. In spite of it, he was able to move his awareness out of this limiting belief into the stellar regions. There he experienced the motion of the cosmos and recreated it for others to "see." This is a clear example of a shift in focus.

Does this mean that you all need to be artists in order to do this? You are all artists every moment, so get excited about the fact that you are creating whatever is going on before you. You are taking your consciousness, dipping it into pure awareness, and painting every moment with those brushstrokes of creation. How do you want it to look? Create it the way you want it to be. What are you going to use? You are going to use pure awareness combined with consciousness, which produces form. It is the very simplest formula of all. *Awareness plus concentrated consciousness equals form.*

You are the medium of consciousness. *You are awareness manifesting as consciousness.* I want you to get the distinction and begin to feel both of these realities within you. You do not have to leave consciousness to know awareness, because anything that has been created in consciousness has used the substance of awareness to do it. Please follow this. Every creation has as much awareness in it as any other creation, and if you keep judging good creation/bad creation, good idea/bad idea, you are going to miss the point. The point is not to make better and better creations, but to understand the delight and spontaneous joy of being in this moment in your life.

Mother Teresa was a wonderful, living example of this. For four hours in the morning, she was on her knees praying. Most of the time there was no awareness of her small self, no awareness of body, no awareness of mind or emotion. There was just awareness. The face of the world changed because of this one small woman. Where do you think that little dynamo got her power? In those hours, when she was pure awareness, her physical form became filled with the creative energy of pure awareness. The things she thought about materialized, and it is because she, Mother Teresa, became creative energy in motion. She took the focus out of herself and placed it in what she called the Heart of God, what I call Pure Awareness, and permeated her entire being with it. Things happened to her as if by magic. *She* was a walking miracle, and *you* can be a walking miracle.

Get excited about awareness. Get excited about this consciousness. The place we're talking about is not far away and hard to find. With practice you can become aware of Awareness instantly. When you begin to feel the creative, dynamic substance of that kind of power, it becomes addictive, so addictive that it overrides all other addictions, all other desires. If you want to do God's will, plug in to where God's will is.

*Out of pure
awareness came
an explosion of
power, the
delightful wave
of consciousness
you have been
riding ever since.*

9

The Spirit of Our Joining

SAN CRISTOBAL, NEW MEXICO

Day One
In Relationship to Each Other and the Divine

When we begin to discuss deep, personal relationships, we are led to talk about unconditional love, because that is the eventual goal. Unconditional love cannot be experienced without help from the Source of love Itself. With that help, it is possible one day to realize you have left possessive, dependent love behind.

Many of you feel that this kind of deep love is beyond your reach until you "fix" yourself and your life. This will never happen. You will never be fully content with yourself and your life when you view it through your ego. What will make your life beautiful and complete is to recognize the deep undercurrent of true love that is always present in Life Itself. It is a love that comes out of the Source of Being and moves through everything you have created. It is that deep motion, always present, that I want you to recognize and experience.

You have all gone through the endless ups and downs that accompany what I would call *personal* love. You make rules and then you break them. You make new ones and you break those. Then you get angry when other people break their rules, and you retaliate by breaking yours, and so it goes. We don't have to spend a lot of time today discussing that kind of romantic dance. You have all lived it, not only in this lifetime, but in many other lifetimes as well. What we are going to do is present various ways for you to open up to unconditional love, and let it make itself felt within you. This will provide an opportunity for you to experience a very different type of relationship.

Unconditional love is the word we will use when we talk about a sense of absolute well-being, wonder, and awe that *comes out of you* and affects *everything* you see, think, or do. You will find that everything is meaningful and appropriate, while no one or no thing is special in the sense of "better than." The Buddhists call this "equal vision." You will sense the value in all things and find that one thing can be experienced with the same awe and gratitude as anything else.

$\phi\ \phi\ \phi$

Love is not just a thought; love is a physical sensation. It is a motion within the physical body that produces a wondrous warmth and sense of well-being, in the face of *anything* that might be happening. Some of you who are serious about your spiritual seeking will immediately run into difficulty around the statement, "within the physical body," because many "spiritual paths" deny the physical. This often gives rise to the feeling that the spiritual goal you are reaching for has to be done in spite of your physical body, or that the body must somehow be put aside for a spiritual experience to unfold.

Well, my friends, have you noticed lately that you all have bodies? Every one of them has its own distinctive feel, its own distinctive harmony, its own distinctive essence of being. Your physical body is a uniquely magnificent entity. When you first decided to experiment with the physical body on the Earth plane, you also decided it could be used to experience the deep upwelling pleasure of feeling the presence of God's Love. To do this, you must first be *in* your bodies. Many of you spend long periods of time totally unaware that you even have one. Some of you live in your minds, and some of you even live somewhere in space, "spaced out," as you say. When you begin to understand how important it is to feel life in your body, you will find ways to make that happen.

One way is through music. Take a few minutes to play some music you really like. As you do, simply experience that music in your body. Pay attention to the kinds of feelings that come into you as you listen. Feel what sound is like. If people or events come to mind, acknowledge them, but don't dwell on them. Listen, with no judgment; just simply "be" in the midst of whatever comes up. Let the music lead you back into your physical body.

Pause.

Your ego would like you to believe that love is complicated. It wants to convince you that you have to go through many, many trials in order to become worthy enough to be in a state of love. Do not be deceived! The more complex you make the process, the longer it will take you to allow yourself to feel the love that is already present. You have all had moments where you've experienced deep love. Those moments are difficult to maintain when they are shattered by the arrival of judgment, perceived differences, feelings of superiority and inferiority—*separation*. With the arrival of separation, the feeling of love seems to disappear. What has happened to that feeling?

♪ ♪ ♪

Let's say you meet someone and find yourself enchanted by this person. Deep within you something moves. You feel, not just excitement, but a sense of being comfortable, of being safe, of being in the presence of something so important and so special that you find yourself willing to share your life with the person you think gives you these feelings. When you meet someone whose energy field moves you in such a way, some aspect of your soul, the God-part of you, responds. It is a recognition of the deep similarity between you. *All* souls are one, and you have seen that place where separation has no part. It is a place of total hope from which you say, "In the presence of this one, I will see and know that which is my best, that which is my highest, that which is my most loving. In the presence of this person, I can be my unguarded, true self."

In those early days, weeks, and months of the relationship, that feeling is built upon. Here is a person you can share everything with: your victories, your defeats, your pains, your joys, your hopes, your delights, your expectations of yourself and life. All of it wells up and blends with this other one, who, from the depths of their being, shares who they are, who they have pretended to be, and who they hope to be. In the presence of each other, you both find yourselves more forgiving. Things that would, in the past, agitate you terribly fade into the background when you have this love in your heart. It's a marvelous, nonjudgmental openness. In loving each other, you begin to love other people as well. You become more allowing, gentler, kinder, more understanding, and more lovable yourself. These are truly magic moments.

In this meeting, something real has happened. I think it is very silly to say that these feelings are just some kind of prelude to a sexual contact that is simply nature's way of producing more children. Do you really think that biology is the only reason you have this feeling? I doubt it, and I think you doubt it! This coming together is a moment of recognition, when the possibility arises that there may be one person who will find enough value in you to stay steady in your life, thereby giving you the opportunity to find out who you really are. That is a good definition of love at its best!

Then one day, perhaps without even knowing where it comes from, there arises in your mind a judgment. "Hmm," says the lover about the beloved, "I don't think I like what is happening. I think it might be a little uncomfortable to live with that characteristic for the rest of my life." At this point nothing is said, but the moment that that first small judgment comes in, you begin a process that you may be stuck with for the rest of your relationship. The process is, judgment leads to doubt, which leads to more judgment, which then accumulates over the years. Of course, the other person is in the same process. So at the very earliest stages, this separation begins to arise and will continue if nothing comes in to break the pattern.

At the start of the relationship, when the soul began to move toward a partnership of deep union, that yearning was so powerful that it was able to silence this judgmental little voice. But the little voice is speaking quietly in the background all the time, whispering things like, "He or she didn't do it right, didn't do it quickly enough," or "My beliefs or family or background are just a little more right than his or hers." This mostly unnoticed judgmental process continues against others and against self.

When this powerful, new love energy wells up, the small, insistent, nagging ego-voice seems to cease. Remember this, because it is where your hope lies. It is possible to begin to silence the ego voice by getting in touch with how you felt when love first sprang up in your heart. Most people, however, try to find another person to feel this with instead of trying to find what once was. You can move from person to person your whole life, but eventually you will run out of energy. It takes a lot of time and effort to keep that game going, so if you are in a relationship where the glow has subsided, you might find it useful to stay put and work with what you have. That feeling can be rediscovered in whoever you are with, if you are both willing to do it.

The original spontaneous explosion is the feeling of a presence of Light within you, the Light that is always there. It doesn't take a love affair to ignite it, but it is certainly one way to have it happen. Historically, and as a culture, you have given other people the power to ignite that Light, and often it is through "falling in love." When you "fall in love," all you do is ignite the fire of love that was always within you.

But there is a problem buried in all of this. *You have identified the other person as necessary for this process.* Without that person, your loving response is not the same. Where you get caught is in believing that the other person is necessary for this process to continue. The minute this belief takes over, fear enters the mind, the fear that if you lose this person, you lose the wonderful feeling. Fear says that one is not possible without the other! If you look closely at your relationships, you might find that you love the feeling of loving *more* than you love the person. If you had a choice of feeling the love, or the person staying without the feeling, which would you pick? Please think about this carefully, because it is essential that you grasp that *it's the feeling you really want.* The person who helps you light the fire *does not have to stay* for you to continue to be warmed by it. They can stay and share it with you, but the warmth does not have to leave if they choose to go.

A feeling of desperation arises with the belief that this incredible feeling of love can only be present when you are with the other person. This desperation leads you to manipulate the situation to make sure they remain. You have found your own private stash of happiness, and you don't want to lose it! It's an elixir that makes you feel expanded, excited, and exalted, and you want to protect it at almost any cost. Fear takes over and runs through the length of the relationship. You are in pain, and they are in pain. The Light gets covered over and is rarely seen. In some cases, it is not seen at all. But the two of you keep going back, trying to recapture the feeling, without really knowing how. Finally one of you, consciously or unconsciously, says, "I don't think it's going to work. I don't think we're going to feel that Light again." So one or the other leaves in search of someone who can help get the Light back, and both are left with a feeling of having failed.

Instead of following this pattern yet again, let's try something different. Begin by remembering the truth. The truth is: *You are the one who turns on the Light.* That Light in you recognizes God in the other, and in that explosive realization, you see who they really are. They are pretending to be a limited human being, but in that moment, you know they are not. In your eyes, their mask dissolves and you see them exalted in the Light of Love. And it is *you* who has done it, *you* who has experienced it. There's something deep, mysterious, and wonderfully exciting and expansive moving inside of you. And through this process of feeling it, you can know, experience, and remember the Light. Someone came into your life, and you saw the Light of God reflected in them.

Those of you who took vows of commitment meant them. You weren't in some kind of hypothetical situation when you said, "I am ready to give my life, not to serve the ego of you, but to serve what I have seen slip through the bars of separation. In one magic, God-given moment, I have seen you; and that is the you I pledge to love forever." Do you all remember? There are very few of you who don't know that, and it's a blessed thing. So whatever the circumstances are now, whether you stayed or left your relationship, remember that the real wonder is the gift of your loving.

$\phi \phi \phi$

So what is to be done about the "fall from grace," the falling out of love? Please take out your paper and pencil and put in big letters at the top, "My Filters." Remember, a filter is a set of beliefs that will only allow you to see the places where you and your partner, parent, child, or friend, do not join—the places where you disagree. The filter is made up of this selective vision and only allows you to see what separates.

The object of this exercise is to get in touch with these filters. Start writing a list of short sentences about the judgments you have against the person or against yourself about them. This is important, because this list of filters is what you are viewing the other person through, and is the cause of your separation from them. These filters keep you from uniting, and the first step out of the situation is to see it exactly as it is. That is why honesty at this stage is crucial.

Pause.

Whether you are conscious of it or not, you enter into love affairs because you are seeking God. Every advance toward unifying with another human being is an attempt to get past places of separation so you can experience wholeness. In its most loving terms, *a relationship is two people who are both looking for God and who wish to enjoy each other as they move toward this inner goal.* The reason having someone in your life works so well for this is because they are always "right under your nose." When you look at them, you really think you are seeing someone separate. You think this person has a particular background, personality, set of problems, and actions not always pleasing to you, the observer. But the joke of it is, my friends, *you are looking at yourself!*

The most devastating thing I could tell your ego is that *what you see out there is you.* And while you are feeling your "oneupmanship," your superiority, the person you are looking at is also feeling theirs. But through all of this, there is an amazing opportunity for you to recognize that you have created a mirror to see yourself reflected in. Your ego tells you this is not so, that you are unique and separate, that what is outside is not you. It may help to remember that everyone else also believes they are the unique and separate one, and that you also are not them.

Pay particular attention to the things "outside of you" that you actively dislike. This can tell you a lot about those things that trigger your judgmental responses. If someone leaves their socks out and you don't mind socks being left out, then socks won't matter. If, however, you don't like socks being left out, that is all you will see when you enter the room. The person may have left you three dozen roses, but if their socks are on the floor, the roses disappear and only socks are left. This is an example of a filter working against you.

You enter into every moment with your filters in place. That means *you will see what you want to see and what you expect to see.* You will *not see what is really going on.* Once you come to realize this truth, you will begin to see how you have been collecting a list of grievances; and these are what you have been focusing on. You will find that you are no longer looking at the other person's beauty, strength, courage, love, or understanding. You are looking *to find those things that will justify the view of them you have created in your mind,* but these are *your* judgments, and the conclusions you draw from them are *yours!* You can consciously turn this around by looking for what attracted you to them in the first place. It certainly wasn't all the things you now judge against.

The idea that you cannot sustain an ongoing feeling of love in your heart for another person is illusory. People who are in love are in the presence of the ever-Present Love that is always there, that does not come and go. It is constant, and they get there by using every moment of their day to *look for* and *find* love. If you are looking for a relationship where you can get to be right, to be better, to be separate, *that* is what you will find. If you start looking for the Light within your relationships, *that* is what you will find. Whatever you may think your relationships are for, your inner Being uses them to find the God-Light.

If you are not feeling totally alive, filled with peace, joy, and love, you are in the presence of an energy that filters out the Light of both your Beings. You have two people with Light in their hearts and a shadow that plays between them. It is up to you whether or not you choose to remove the filters of past fear and future judgment toward any other person. The rewards are great, for when you see the Light in them, you will also see the Light in yourself.

§ § §

I would like to tell you of a very wonderful cartoon Mary-Margaret saw recently. It is a picture of two fishbowls that are so close together that they are touching. Inside each fishbowl is a fish facing the other. Underlying the picture is a caption, "What happened to all of the fun we were going to have together?" This is a perfect analogy of what a filter can do to a relationship. Symbolically, we are dealing with an illusory fishbowl of separation. The fishbowls represent the ego, and are created by the external senses. They are, in a sense, your cocoon of separation. When you look at each other, you see the separation. In addition, you see your own bowl to such an extent that you rarely see the other person's bowl at all, let alone the other fish. And this is what you call "being in a relationship."

That sense of being isolated and alone, unable to be seen by another, comes from living in a fishbowl constructed from your opinions and beliefs about life, love, and intimacy. These begin very early in your life. To be dependent on someone is appropriate in infancy. If you are one week old, you don't say, "Thanks, Mom, you've done enough. I'll take it from here." You say,

"I don't want you to leave, and if you do, you had better leave a substitute because I can't handle this by myself." The infant knows that it is not capable of taking care of itself. Later in life, this response is no longer appropriate, but many people never create a new response, so they are left with the message: "Safety and love come from outside." Now you have to depend on someone besides yourself to get those things. What is really needed is to begin looking inside yourself to find the Light.

You can find endless ways to do this, whether it's being in nature, jogging a mile, meditating, listening to music, or whatever works for you. The power of that Light will warm up your heart. The filters will melt so love can flow. It is your own interconnected network of pain that keeps you from opening your heart. The name of the game in love affairs seems to be, "How can I take a minimum of risk and still get a maximum of love in return?" This is the ego's statement. But what will happen if you take down all your walls and stand exposed in the light of love? Who will you be, without your fishbowl? There is fear that you will be too vulnerable, but you have forgotten how powerful you are, how full of abundant wisdom, love, and creativity. You have believed yourself to be a limited being, needing other people to help you feel your own God-given Light, power, love, and total bliss. *That is not true,* and as you begin to build your own inner safety by always looking for and remembering that *you* are the Light, that truth will dawn.

Some of you are afraid to join with your partner on a deep level for fear you will be "stuck" with them for life. There is a fear when you love someone that they can control you. So the ego whispers, "Don't love them deeply or you are lost." But I say, if you start loving deeply, you will be free. Love sets you free— to stay and enjoy the dance, or to acknowledge that you both need something else. To love is freedom. Not to love is bondage. That is exactly the opposite of what your ego wants you to believe.

When you allow yourself to truly feel love without exception, you will begin to see that love does not bind you. It is a feeling of deep release. If you want to be free of your emotional messes, love more, not less. In that loving, you will become so empowered, so full of energy, so full of life, that you will make life-creating choices, not ego-based responses. Love opens up new worlds where everybody wins, and where more love is created.

$$\text{\textit{\J} \text{ \J} \text{ \J}}$$

When you find yourself in difficult relationships, your ego tries to convince you that the other person is creating the abrasive parts of your shared environment. Yet you must both live in that environment, so why not learn to use it to increase your love and light, rather than your pain and resentment? A good way to begin this process is to get away from that environment for a while. Those of you who live alone will find this a revealing exercise as well, because when you return, you will have a chance to see just what you have created. Stop at the door and put down the luggage. Wait. Feel your environment with your heart, with all your senses. Take it in. Then quickly jot down your impressions about it. Is it pleasing, and if not, why not? How does it smell? Is it too empty or too filled with "things"? Write down how you feel about this place called home. What would you change, and most of all, *what does it say about you?*

Remember that your home is just a reflection of the environment inside you. You have created this extension of yourself with your thoughts, feelings, decisions, and actions. If your home is too cluttered, don't stop by saying, "My house is too cluttered." Be willing to go deeper. There is something behind that observation. Does it reflect a basic belief that having things brings happiness? Or is it a belief in scarcity? Is it a belief such as, "There isn't enough to go around," or "I'm not worth spending money on," or "Comfort isn't important"? As you use your ability for introspection to go deeply within yourself and examine your world from that point of view, you will begin to experience power over *your* world. The power comes through your growing awareness of what is really in front of you and understanding what connects you to it. You come to understand yourself.

You do all this by paying attention to how things feel in your body. You learn to read your own energy with your intuition. Most of you are reading your energy with your mind, which is not as effective. Your minds have been conditioned so you all have a lot of the same thought patterns about many, many things. The way to find out how you run your energy is to *feel* it. It's part of your language—"How do you feel about this?" rather than, "What do you think about this?" You can practice becoming aware of what your energy is saying to you. Pay attention to what it tells you when you are in the presence of other people. You are not the same person in each situation, and it will become easy to read the difference.

𝄞 𝄞 𝄞

Close your eyes and visualize someone you feel you have difficulty with. Visualize their body, the expression on their face. Really see them. As you do, pay close attention to how your own body feels. Are you hot, cold, uncomfortable, shy, embarrassed, angry, hurt? Then, after a few moments, visualize someone who you feel very loving towards, and again pay attention to how your own energy feels around them. Is it soft, gentle, excited, open, relaxed?

Pause.

These different bodily sensations give you important clues as to what is going on. You may have felt your body contract when you visualized someone who is difficult for you. There may be a tightness, shortness of breath; or you may not even be able to see very well. This is your body saying, "I don't want to see them." or "I don't want to see this situation again." Your body takes care of you, so the muscles in your eyes contract, and you literally "can't see what's in front of you." The eyes are a part of your filter system and help to keep you safe. So pay attention, and quietly ask yourself if the present situation is really as dangerous as the signals indicate, or is the past coming into the present? When you take hold of your energy like this, you begin to feel much less fearful, far less vulnerable, and more "in charge."

One of you has described feeling a prickly sensation when visualizing a person you have difficulty with. That sensation is a barrier you have purposely created. Like the porcupine, you defend yourself behind your prickly spines. You may find yourself backing out the door or getting very stiff, silent, withdrawn, and defensive when you are in this person's presence. That prickly response in your body is what can show you exactly how you feel. Your mind translates what the body reveals. If you feel your energy shooting off in all directions, you would say you were "off center." There is no centered point because you feel yourself "all over the place." Often, this is because you don't want to be where you are. All of a sudden you feel unsafe in the presence of this person's energy field, and you want to leave. These feelings are the way the body lets you know it is not safe. The body will also tell you the opposite. When your body relaxes, safety is usually present. Much of the fear comes from the past.

One of your jobs in a relationship is to provide a safe environment where relaxation is possible for both of you. If you are in a place where you are constantly having to struggle for a sense of "rightness," always asking yourself, *Am I right, am I wrong? Am I good, am I bad? Am I appropriate, am I not?*, then you will never be able to relax. Many of you come from households you never felt safe enough to relax in. It could be a home where one of the adults changed partners a lot or where you were shuttled between your mother and father. Things may have been stable for a while, then suddenly things would change and you would be left looking for a place of safety. This might make you wary of change and people. It may take a lot of years to learn to trust people enough to feel relaxed with them. How do you do it? By becoming aware of the feelings in your body when people are present. What is the energy saying? Does your old response still make sense? Are you still in the jeopardy you once were, or are you now safe? If you are not a child anymore and you are in a relationship you don't like, you do have the choice to leave it. Don't underestimate the power the enforced environment of your early years has over you.

$ $ $

You cannot control the world. There are going to be people in it who don't like you, no matter how sweet and wonderful you are. There are going to be hostile, angry, hateful, resentful, negative, overwhelming, pushy, arrogant responses from people who trample your feelings and stomp on your sense of self. This world is made up of many people who are afraid and who respond to fear in "negative" ways. You cannot change this, and as spiritual seekers, you must not even attempt to. Staying away from them is not the solution. So, what is?

The process needed is really opposite of what the ego would tell you. The ego says, "Push them away. Protect yourself. Get them out of your life." But you have to do the exact opposite. *You have to take the feeling in.* You do not just meditate in holiness; you meditate in wholeness. Wholeness means accepting all parts of yourself, and all parts of your life. So you take it all into your heart. Your heart is a crucible of power filled with flamelike Light. So you take this piece of lead, encompassing leadlike feelings of anger, resistance, resentment, judgment, and you actually place them in the crucible of the heart. By that I mean, keep taking it in, taking it in, until you get a "felt-sense" of the whole situation.

Now look, my friends, this is not just a two-minute exercise on a Saturday afternoon. You are going to have these uncomfortable feelings for much of your lives, so you've got to make a decision about what to do with them. Either you go to your mind, endlessly thinking about them; or you come to realize that *thinking about them often increases their power.* As you add your thoughts to the existing problem, each one increases the amount of energy in it. So get out of your mind and begin the transmutation in your heart. Transmutation of energy is an alchemical process. You can bring those leadlike feelings into your heart, and allow the fire, which you know as love, to change them into something else. You don't even know how it's going to work, or *if* it's going to work. But do it anyway. *How can you possibly know until you try it?*

Every moment of your life is a Divine gift and an opportunity to fly Home in an instant. Every moment you stand on the brink of experiencing your true nature. How could you not be? It is Who You Always Are. Given this, I wish to discuss another aspect of relationship. It is called *mirroring* and can become your great friend, instead of something you want to run from. It's a skill to encourage in yourself. As with any skill, the more you practice it, the more you will understand it.

The ego would love to take you to the negative aspect of mirroring. It does this by constantly asking what horrible thing in you is being mirrored by this horrible thing in front of you. You *must* realize that no matter how "horrible" the something in front of you looks, it is there to mirror *some aspect of God-Consciousness* back to you. Why God-Consciousness? *Because it's all God.* So first of all you say, "Here comes God, pretending to be whoever or whatever is in front of me. This is an aspect of the Divine coming to teach me, so let's wake up and pay attention."

Then the second step is to go back and check the body. Quit thinking and start feeling. Stop the mental processing. Your mental beliefs and emotional responses will take you out of the moment to someplace no longer in the present. *It is the body that is in the present, so it is the body that has the answer.* Stop and ask yourself what you are feeling as you stand there. Allow yourself to relax. Don't start pushing your feelings away because you don't like them. Do the opposite. Open up and become relaxed. "Here comes God. Here comes the Divine in a form that is difficult for me. All right, God, what are we going to do about this?"

Remember, as you are looking in your "mirror," you are accessing the information through your body, right now, this moment. Then very gently pull into the picture that Divine part of *you* that understands what you are looking at. You do this by asking to be shown what you deeply need to know about this mirror so you can then see clearly. How would that Divine part of you view this? You are accessing the most powerful place of knowing that you, as a human consciousness, have available. You cannot easily still the mind, and your emotions are in constant flux. But you can render the body still in an instant, and in that stillness, receive knowings and promptings. It is in this stillness that you will find the answers. Understanding will appear where confusion once stood.

$ $ $

Here is an exercise where you can choose to take a risk. If you are in a primary relationship, sit down opposite each other, face to face. If you are not, choose someone else, since you are always in a relationship with whoever is in front of you. If your partner is not present, or if it's someone in your life you would like to work with who isn't with you at this time, just create them in your consciousness. Then, as you both become quiet, allow yourselves to feel the energy that is moving between you.

Don't analyze. Don't think things such as, *Since we are all one, I feel oneness with this person.* That may be true. but it's not what we are ready for yet. We are trying to find that place in you where you give and receive energy. Remember, all you are doing is finding out, "What does this person feel like? How does my body respond to this person?" Is the energy in motion, or has it locked somewhere? Gently be aware of all of it, allowing the feelings to play back and forth without expectations. Stay with it. If you wish, your partner doesn't even have to know what you are doing. You can do this exercise when you are sitting together reading, watching the universal mandala of the television, or lying in bed. The energy between you will show you who they really are.

You are so used to listening to your thoughts to get an idea of whether or not you enjoy being in the presence of someone that some of you are going to be very surprised at what happens when thought is absent. Your relationship may have arguments as part of it, so you think you are not suited for each other. But you may be deeply attuned in your hearts. The mental manifestation is not a true indication of what is really going on. Some people say they fight like cats and dogs, yet when I look at them, their hearts are singing along, having a wondrous little dance together. I see other people who talk sweetly about how much they love each other, and there is very little connection between them.

Energy doesn't lie. As you pay attention to what is between you, allowing your thoughts to subside, you will begin to experience the "true nature" of the other person. You will begin to feel their courage, their hopes, their yearnings, their love, their willingness. *You will begin to feel that they are basically the same as you!* You will feel your oneness, your similarly, your unity. And then, in one glorious moment, they will no longer be "someone separate who you need to understand." You will understand them because they are you!

$$\delta \quad \delta \quad \delta$$

Day Two
We Are Not Who We Think We Are

So then, good morning. Let us see if we can spend today fine-tuning and expanding on some of the material we covered yesterday. We have been talking about the different aspects of relationship. You call one of the difficult aspects "being backed up," meaning that the accumulation of anxiety, tension, and stress between you is what you see as wrong.

But what is really causing your pain? Perhaps it is the result of withholding your love. When your body is torqued with pressure, headache, tension, and pain, do you withhold any of this from your friends? No. People are usually aware when you are having trouble. Your stress is obvious. It shows in your body, in how you look, in what you say and how you say it, and to whom. You might even find yourself saying things such as, "I have this problem, and because I have this problem, it's your problem to solve my problem." There is nothing stuck about such expression. But when you have released this tension, often the problem remains.

The solution to these "problems" is to set your love in motion. In the moment when you would prefer to express yourself in unloving ways that would most distance you from your lover or whoever else is in front of you, *try the opposite.* Open up and allow love energy to move through you. I know this is the last thing you want to do. It is the last thing, but it would help tremendously if it was the first. If you want out of the tension and stress that your body, emotions, or mind build, there is only one place to go, and that is to a higher energy frequency. *You cannot go to a lower frequency and expect to feel better.* You will have a momentary release, then the tension will return. So you must follow the law that says, move to a higher rate of vibration if you want to find a way to explode out of these painful thoughts and emotions. The highest frequency you will ever find is the God-vibration, *which is the vibration of love.*

With love, you will find that talking together is better than yelling at one another, and understanding the other's point of view is better than talking. Let us say you have become aware of a problem and you think you understand the situation. You could then say, "Look, I've got to talk to you because this is coming up for me, and talking will help me to be clear about it." So you present your view with the open willingness to also hear their view of things. But you don't just talk and listen. You talk and listen, and at the same time, expand your love into the space between you. This brings in the higher vibration of love, which gives you the opportunity to really join with the other person in understanding a new way of seeing the situation.

It is wonderful that so many of you attempt to work out your relationships for as long as you do. It is a real testimony to true friendship when two people constantly keep trying to see each other clearly. But some of you feel you cannot do this at the moment, so you turn away and run. You may run out of the house, out of the relationship, or just out of your feelings. Perhaps you run because you have failed in the past and don't see how this time it can be any different. Perhaps you feel that there is no way for two such different points of view to ever find common ground. But different points of view can *always* come together if love is brought into the moment.

The moment when you are most unlovable and nonreceptive to love, when you are the most isolated and most imploded, is exactly the time you are being asked to bring in the love. The methods may differ, but the process is the same. The process is to take the energy field of love, which is the only thing that can heal the situation, and bring that feeling into the moment. You may find this very hard to do, because those are the moments you are most afraid to be loving, but look carefully and you may find that something else is present along with your fear and unwillingness.

Love is also there, and *love comes when you call. You* must do the inviting, and often you must do it just at the moment when you least want to.

♪ ♪ ♪

We heard yesterday from a lady who lost her son six years ago, and she says that in doing the meditation, it seems to her that the pain of it is still in every fiber and cell of her body. I would like to address this issue because it fits in with what we have been saying. The pain in the body is caused by the belief that she has really lost someone. It's a deep belief that, because the beloved is no longer seen, he is gone. That is not true. But I could say this forever and it would not convince her. What can convince her is an experience of the truth. The truth is that you are always connected to anyone you have ever loved! You are connected to them *by* that love. You feel grief because you *have* loved. Is it possible to keep the love and release the grief?

I have a suggestion that may help. Take a few minutes to fix the person clearly in your mind. Make the image of them as real as you can. Then allow yourself to feel love, not only for the person, but love itself moving deeply inside you. Stay with it and keep feeling the love, letting it grow and expand. Love is a fire that burns, and it can burn away the grief. Do this over and over. Flood the image, and flood your body with love. This is inner work on the deepest level, and it will take time. Do what you can. If you find that you are afraid to do anything more than just say the word love, *do that for a while and it will grow. Just begin where you are.*

Love knows its own name. It knows when it's being called. Speak it as if it's a mantra. **Stay with the intention of feeling the love!** *As you hold the image of the beloved in your mind, feel the love, and hold your emotional body steady. It's the* **emotional** *body that begins to vibrate with the remembrance of the pain.*

Pain is present, but much deeper and resounding more clearly is the vastness of love.

When you begin to feel the love, you will also begin to feel a *union* between that person and yourself. You really will be joined, and you will begin to know this on the deepest cellular level. This is important because it's the cells that hold the grief. It is the physical body that *holds* the tension that *holds* the pain. And when you begin to feel the union of your love with the image of the beloved, you will relax. The cells in your body will relax and open, and the grief will start to dissipate. What will remain is the love.

All of you have felt grief, but many of you feel guilty about the weight of such feelings. You feel your grief small compared to someone who has had a *real* loss, such as the death of a child. So you try to shake yourselves out of it by scolding yourselves. "Come on now, stop feeling so bad. You have only lost a love affair. Look what others have gone through." You scold yourselves because you think you do not have a bona fide reason to feel such pain, yet you do, and now you have added guilt to it and find yourself in a seemingly hopeless mess.

Of course you hurt, and one of the essentials to healing is to honor the fact that you are in pain. Do not slide away from that truth. You are in pain. Acknowledge it, and allow your body to feel it. Find out where in your body the pain accumulates, and fully feel the pain in those places. Then do the thing that is the hardest: *Relax into the pain.* Hold steady; don't run. Be fully aware of what you are feeling. You know pain is there, but *so is the love.* And the more you concentrate on that love, the less often you will feel the pain. Love always softens the anguish. For those of you who are good at visualizing, stop and *see* your heart opening and the love pouring out. For others of you, stop and remember that you *want* to feel love, instead of whatever else you are feeling.

God is the quick fix of the universe. There is no question about it. When you are so enmeshed with someone and there is no time to sit down and go through each point of your disagreement, when the space between you needs immediate changing, when you want to create a harmonious environment *now*; you have to do something fast. So don't let your ego run the moment; allow the light of your being to begin to move through you. *Allow* that love to be present. Don't *think* it, don't cave in on your emotions; just remember that the Light of your joyful Being is always present, and relax into It. Start practicing, and you will begin to see it happen. Are there any questions?

৶ ৶ ৶

Participant: I have a fear that I will take what you are suggesting and repress my emotions.

My friend, your emotional body, anyone's emotional body, is always present and in a constant state of motion. It is part of being human. You need to be aware of those responses since they are a part of who you are, and acknowledge their presence. Name the feeling, if possible. Really experience what is going on. Therapy is helpful because it encourages you to feel what you have been afraid to feel, and helps you not to run away. But therapy is just one step. There must come a moment when you decide to drop the past by bringing in love. You need to know you have the choice of loving and moving on. But this stage only comes when you have spent sufficient time feeling your feelings and are ready to create things differently.

If you are in therapy, I would suggest you do the following after every session. Spend a little time filling yourself with what you really want to feel. Love? Peace? Guiltless awareness? You will benefit greatly. Go to a therapist who believes that there is a greater power than the limited mind. Without that transmuting power of greater awareness, nothing in therapy really changes. You do not call this power in so you don't have to feel; you call it in to help you feel *more than your limited self.* When you call on love, its power goes through you and into the situation leaving you stronger, and the situation clearer. You feel more alive, more ready to face the next moment. So don't "stuff your feelings," but after you have felt and named them, let this wonderful love energy fill you. Let it heal you. Let it heal you by filling all the places where you have let something go.

When you look at anyone outside yourself or at any event taking place in the world, try to remember that *you are in the presence of the Light of God.* Love is the true nature of all things. If you are willing to keep remembering that, the process of clarifying and dissolving anything that keeps you from that awareness will begin. When you remember in this way, you will come to know that anything you see other than Light is temporary; a momentary, transient disturbance that rises and falls, comes and goes. Keep focused on what is really there, under the camouflage of shifting perceptions and beliefs.

You believe you are your bodies. You believe so deeply in karma and reincarnation that it is difficult to drop the past and just become aware that Light is *always* meeting Light. And when Light meets Light, *greater Light* is the result. I promise, if you remember that all is God in whatever way you can, your difficulties will be clarified. The Light will come. The Light will deepen, and the love will be manifest. The vibration of love is what keeps you safe. You may think it is other people, money, health, or power, but in the end, it is the high vibration of love that is your safe harbor. Love shows you the true nature of things, of people and events. You all want to feel safe within your body, within your emotions, within your mind, within your heart, within your life, and within your world. It is your birthright to feel safe, and it is love that makes this all possible. And that love is ever-present.

ψ ψ ψ

What keeps you from relaxing into the love of God is your *fear*. Your list of fears is endless, and those fears result in more tension and less openness. An enlightened one has, at the deepest level, relaxed into their essence. You call it "surrendering." It's the final, ultimate letting go, not letting go to something, just *letting go*. Stay in your body, alive and aware of emotions, tensions, pressures, whatever might be going on. Then without thinking about it, without having to understand it, release it. *You created this pressure; therefore, you can release it.* In relation to each other, you have done nothing wrong. Your egos have gone through endless permutations on various themes, and various things have happened as a result. Exchanges have been made, and energy has moved back and forth between you. All of that is true, but the "I" of you, that which is your true nature, has done none of it. It has gone on, moving beautifully, perfectly, and harmoniously through every moment of every dream you have dreamed.

When you say, "I have to love more," you are talking about doing something. If you would drop those words out of your awareness and substitute something such as, "I can allow more love," it will make all the difference in the world. You cannot *do* love. You just release the blocks that keep it from flowing. Love is an incredible, dynamic, empowering energy that moves through everything; and in allowing love into any situation, your choices *get made by love*. It is not your mind thinking about what love would have you do, but rather love itself doing what needs to be done.

You hold the gates closed tightly against love because you are afraid of pain. You have stood resolutely in the face of your pain for lifetimes and you are still here, facing it again. I am not asking you to stand against the pain, but to be open and *dare* to love, in the midst of the pain. *Dare* to allow the love to move. It is the vibration of the pain that keeps the floodtide of love from moving in greater and greater frequency through the body. You *can* allow the pain to dissolve. It will not move if you keep saying you haven't understood it enough or talked about it enough or looked at it long enough. You must take the risk of allowing yourself, in the midst of your pain, to say, "No, this pain is not who I am. That is not the truth of my being!"

$$\vartheta \quad \vartheta \quad \vartheta$$

God mirrors Itself back a hundredfold. I have always told you, when you take one step, God takes a hundred. Those are words, but they are also a reality. When someone is doing something that is difficult for you, you can take a step by saying, "That is *not* who they are. Their fear has made them perceive things in a way that is frightening to them. In their fear, they have attacked." Wait and feel what returns. They may still be doing whatever it was that gave you difficulty, but you have taken a step toward unity, so something different will come back to you. They don't even know what they are giving you. It comes through them to you because that difficulty is *not who they are.* If they have forgotten, you remember for them, because God is constantly remembering for you. *While you have forgotten, the Divine has never forgotten who or what you really are.*

No matter how dark your path or how far you have wandered, a part of you has never forgotten. If you can just remember for an instant that the faces you are presenting each other are not who either of you are, the love will be mirrored back a hundredfold, a thousandfold. Then one day, the mirror will be empty. They will not be there, and you will not be there. There will be nothing but the One. Your willingness to remember that they are filled with the Light of God is what pulls the gift of love out of the ineffable wonder of their being. You bestow the gift on them, and the gift is returned. The giving and receiving are the same. You have created each other for this purpose, to remind each other, "We are not who we think we are."

Using the beauty of your brothers and sisters to accelerate your path is to use them with honor and dignity. The camouflage of the illusion seems alive. But it is the life behind it that is real. It is in everything you see. You created each other for the beautiful, mystical awakening to this. It is an intense undertaking, but remember, your true nature is at peace, open, endlessly, ceaselessly, wondrously open and free—free of pain, free of doubt, free of confusion, and free of fear.

Just relax and become aware that all createdness is One, in and out of form, with each part seemingly different, but really all the same. The Source and the substance are the same. All things were made by God-Consciousness, and there is but One. You exist; therefore, you are That.

10

Meet the Universe

ALBUQUERQUE, NEW MEXICO

One of my jobs is to stretch you as much as I can before the time comes when we no longer have these kinds of dialogues. The idea behind any teaching or set of experiential exercises is to get you so vast that, to use an analogy, you can increase the size of your playground. Your present playgrounds may seem quite small, and there may not be very many toys that still excite you. So I want to use today to excite you about new extensions of consciousness.

§ § §

When you remove yourself from your usual environment and place yourself in a new "playground," you find out new things about yourself. This is one reason we take you on tour to different places around the globe. When you are on a tour or visit new cities, new countries, or new places in nature, you have a head-on collision with your own awareness. You find out immediately where you have fear and where you do not, where you feel pleasure and where you are judgmental, where you have a sense of love for humankind, and where you are repulsed. You will find your "self" around every corner. The point of travel is not so much to visit strange and exotic places, as to discover strange and exotic parts of yourself that you have never understood or had to confront. What happens, for instance, when you find yourself in a Cairo airport, boarding a plane from the same airline with the same flight number that had been hijacked the month before, as happened on our tour to Egypt? Who are you then? What new parts of your awareness do you find, and how do you then respond to them?

$$\text{\$ \$ \$}$$

With this in mind, I would like to begin today by reading a passage from a text by Colin Wilson titled *Beyond the Occult*.[3] The year was 1964, and a friend of Mr. Wilson's was hitchhiking around the world. He was a man who had not undergone any significant amount of so-called spiritual training, but was traveling alone with his own consciousness, experimenting with his awareness. He had been traveling for months, and finally arrived at a place where he could rest.

> I had been through a great deal of emotional turmoil and privation during my travels, and arrived at Cyprus with great relief at having left the scenes of my suffering behind. One evening I was sitting, gazing vacantly at the sea in the afterglow of sunset, having just finished a meal in a little Greek eatery, feeling tranquil and relaxed. I began to feel a strange pressure in my brain. It was as if some deliciously loving hand had slipped numbingly under my skull and was pressing another brain on top of mine. I felt a thrilling liquidity of being, an indescribable sensation, as if the whole universe was being poured into me; or perhaps rather, as if the whole universe was welling up out of

---

[3] Colin Wilson, *Beyond the Occult,* Transworld Publishers Ltd., London, England, 1988.

me from some deep center. My "soul" thrilled and swelled, and my consciousness passed out across the ocean and the land in all directions, through the sky and out into space. Within moments I was among the stars, and the planets and strange entities of space. Somehow I was aware of great beings, millions of miles high, moving in space, through which the stars could be seen. Wave after wave of revelation swept through my whole being, too fast for my normal mind to record, other than the joy and the wonder of it.

We have presented this experience to stretch your belief of what is possible for human consciousness. When we bring forward new concepts such as those that Mr. Wilson's friend experienced, a kind of rapport is established between "you" and the "new idea." Now that you have read this account, you will never be surprised again at the reality of beings millions of miles high. You will not be totally surprised at the capability of one human consciousness to move up and out of his seeming limitations. As you too are experiencing human consciousness, you are also capable of such awakenings.

But do you believe such events are possible for you? If not, how can you develop such a belief? Start with what awareness you have available to you at this moment. Keep inquiring, keep looking within, keep asking to understand limitlessness, and the truth of consciousness will begin to reveal itself to you. Keep wanting to have vaster experiences. Expansion is not only possible, it is inevitable. Expansion is inevitable because it is part of your true nature. You are living on many levels at the same time, and the vast parts of you that are not playing in the reality called human incarnation are constantly moving through you, urging you on. So just keep walking. You *will* awaken.

$ $ $

In our earliest years together, we talked about the great sea of consciousness that contains spherical particles of light. I would like you, right now, to think of yourself as one of those light particles in that sea of consciousness. Imagine yourself as a sphere of moving light. Really see and feel it for a moment. When your focus is in that small sphere, you have the experience of what seems to be an individual self. That is the point from which you view everything. From that point of view, you experience yourself as small and isolated. But you can also withdraw your awareness from that viewpoint and begin to play with the idea of expanding outside your small body, small mind, and small emotions into the sea itself.

Many of the exercises we have you do in workshops are to get you into such an expansion. We ask you to expand to the trees, to the sky, past the planet, to the vastness beyond. We want you to keep stretching. The more you do this, the more you begin to realize you can stretch yourself out of your smallness into something vaster. So much is going on that the relative importance of "you-ness" fades. In the vastness of expansion, smaller things are not going to look so important, nor will they seem to have any ongoing reality.

When you choose to reenter your small, limited awareness, you then reverse the process, but your very cells remember the experience of the vastness. The exhilaration of moving through endless space without fear has become real to your body, mind, and emotions. Excitement replaces fear. What could there be to fear? You are simply awareness experiencing different aspects of itself. The apprehension only comes when you start worrying about what's happening to your body. Don't worry. Once you begin to feel bodily concern, you will find yourself back in your body! There are many possibilities open to you as you gain the ability to leap from small identity to vast identity. And you *can* do it! You will speed the process along by relaxing and settling into your body. Breathe into it. Feel it. Be present in it.

The most helpful tool you have to use from this moment on is the *yearning* to experience something other than your limited consciousness. We have told you, you are not what you *think* you are. You are not your body; you are not your emotions; and you are not your thoughts, although there is an awareness of body, emotions, and thoughts. Trying to define what you are is very difficult, so just for today, let us define what you are as a magnificent and benevolent *potentiality* of consciousness, that decided it wanted to experience something called "you." Holding that idea/desire firmly in place, it moves into the world of form and builds the form you call "you." This consciousness then becomes *aware* of "you" as being that creation, and begins to experience from that point of view. "You" see and feel and think of "you" as that limited form. But that is not the real *"you"*—as you can find out! Just hearing that this is so begins the "finding" potentiality.

If you are willing, there are some very simple things you can do to experience your vast Self. As often as you can, and especially when going into the sleep state, begin to play with your awareness. Push it out until it actually touches the walls of your room and beyond. Just imagine that you are going out until, bonk, you've hit something. And when your mind tells you that you've made all of this up, don't listen. Try again. Remember how Colin Wilson's friend said something came up in him and went out? That "something" is your consciousness released from its limited concept of self. You start that process when you say, "I want to. I am going to begin."

Don't wait for some magic moment in the future. Don't wait for a magic teacher or teaching. *Your present awareness is exactly as vast as you imagine it can be, whether you are conscious of that or not.* When you begin to practice this expansion and can experience moving out, you will soon know the delight of playing with your own awareness. If you are tired of the sameness of your responses, thoughts, and reality, try something new. Mr. Wilson's friend had this experience happen quickly, with overwhelming force. He had no idea what was out there. He just went. That's the kind of expansion you are looking for, isn't it? So practice expansion. Keep pushing. You don't have to worry about going too far out because you will only expand as far as is safe for you. Keep practicing until your limits dissolve. Go out in all directions, just as a balloon does when it's blown up. It is wonderful!

You need to practice this with consistency. Yes. Practice when waiting for someone, standing in line, or whenever you have a few quiet moments. The more you expand into a vastness, the more you will understand what I am talking about. If you don't have enough money, *expand*! If you don't have enough love, *expand*! Give *us* more room in which to join "you." The smaller you get through fear and constriction, the worse it becomes. The more frightened you are about not getting or losing what you have, the more afraid you get, and less fuel becomes available for expansive, spontaneous combustion.

$ $ $

Whether you know it consciously or not, your relationships are an *equal* creation between two people. There are no victims and no "bad guys," and you could know this if you would practice expansion. You become afraid to expand because you are holding on to the old. But this can change. You can begin to have the wonderful experience of knowing you are totally *here*, and *expanded* at the same time. You can be both present in the moment and expanded at the same time. You will realize that there is a larger playground for you both to roam around in. So in the midst of an argument, *expand*. When you do, you expand into potentiality, and potentiality contains the possibility of something new.

Potentiality contains all things, and potentiality simply is. It is another way to talk about God or the Divine. It rests in what could be called the stillness of Awareness. It is that magnificent point of possibility that is everywhere present. It is the created and the uncreated, and that which does the creating and that from which all creation comes. To name it is to speak a lie. To talk about it is to only point at it. To simply *hear* this vast potentiality exists is to begin to move toward it in your consciousness. It is always present, and when you as creator and experiencer of reality *on any level* have a yearning, that potentiality moves toward and interfaces with you. Out of that intimate interface, different areas of consciousness come together and join in creation. That is how thoughts, visions, and forms are created, out of the total Potentiality of the Source. You do not create your reality out of ego desire, but from the deep yearning of your Being, which is Awareness Itself.

When you decide to create yourself as a happy, enlightened, conscious, expansive, endlessly creative human being, your decision and your potentiality begin to intermingle. At the same time, all parts of human consciousness that have ever used the potentiality to create a similar reality are drawn toward you as a magnet attracts another magnet. When you make the statement of the you that you wish to create, you automatically draw on the power of *universal* consciousness to support it. It is a beautiful, helpful, very large and abundant energy field. Use it!

Remember, you create from many other "points of view." Parts of your awareness are millions of miles high. These "Higher Selves" are yet another creation that is filled with potentiality, which in turn creates another, vaster sphere of consciousness. The *only* limitation in your ability to use these creations is your belief that you cannot flow and expand from one part of The Wholeness to another. Awareness is One. You are a part of that One, and knowing this is your destiny on this Earth.

∮ ∮ ∮

Many of you think that the physical plane limits you to a certain kind of vision. I am here to say that that's nonsense. *You* have created this sharing with Bartholomew every month. How did you do it? When enough of you decided you wanted a vaster view of things, you created a way to have that vaster view. So we all come together one Sunday a month, and you pretend that you don't have much wisdom. "You" sit there in the audience, and "I" sit up front and discuss spiritual things. Then you pretend you are getting wiser and more aware, more expanding and loving, when all the time you are already wisdom. Love the expanded vastness Itself. That is the nature of this particular game we are playing together. It is fun, isn't it!

Then why is this "creation" leaving? Because you are ready to create a new game, and you will go on to something bigger. You see, my friends, having allowed yourselves to create this, you *are* bigger, every one of you. You are vaster, so your next creation is going to be *even vaster* than this. That is the law of creation. *You will not go backwards.* You will not create less awareness than this in your own lives. Do not be afraid of any valid teaching leaving you. It only means you are ready for something more exciting, more filled with the potentiality of consciousness. I think most of you have enjoyed this particular creation a lot, and in your enjoyment has come joy to many, many, many parts of consciousness.

So you join your awareness with whatever you think Bartholomew is, one Sunday a month, and you stretch yourselves. Every time you listen to one of the tapes or read one of the books, you stretch yourselves. Don't give Bartholomew the credit. You, as awareness, did it, as *It* does all things. You yearned to be vaster, and this is what you got. But this type of presentation has its limitations, and therefore needs to end. When it does, those of you who care enough about this experience will find that you have access to the same vastness without Mary-Margaret or any person having to be present. You will experience this energy directly, powerfully, intimately. There will be no need for an intermediary.

A large number of you have come together, creating a wonderful song of consciousness. I would like to thank you, because it has allowed "me" to participate in a new way in a creation. From my side, it has been fascinating, exciting, and expansive. And we are not done yet! I want you to understand this particular process of creating so you will know yourself to be a creator of consciousness. Then when you are "on your own," you will find that you are not on your own at all, that what you have done by your dedication to this process is to create a very, very large opening through which you can enter something new. When this creation you have called Bartholomew leaves this particular area of consciousness and expands into a vaster part of the One, you will find the magnet "Bartholomew" *keeps pulling you on!*

If you wish to come along, begin by expanding. When someone is talking to you, expand your awareness through the space between you so that the other person and you share a *spatial* relationship. You will soon realize the space is *filled* with something. That mysterious "something" is the potential we have been talking about. The minute you know this, you become identified, not with your small self, but with this vast potential which then becomes the point of reference from which you meet all others. Just as you and the space are somehow an extension of the same oneness, you will begin to feel that the person in front of you is also part of this oneness. With that experience comes the letting go of your addiction to staying separate. In the end, my friends, the pain of your life is your commitment to feeling separate. Drop that commitment and be free.

From the endless, magnificent stretches of consciousness, that which is the total potentiality of all things, the world enters through you, collectively and individually; and the greater your commitment to having it be a conscious event, the vaster the information you receive can be. We don't have a lot of time left to do this together. Please, practice. Expand, and have fun playing with that greatest of all toys, your consciousness.

11

A Brother's Prayer

ALBUQUERQUE, NEW MEXICO

Good morning, my friends. Today I would like to deal with something we have spoken of before, and which is so important that repetition seems appropriate. The question is: Where do you go for your safety? As you may have noticed, there is a great deal of anxiety building in various parts of your world. You are all familiar with the negative aspects that troubled times can bring, so I would like to focus on the positive possibility that these worldwide difficulties are wonderful opportunities to expand God-Consciousness.

§ § §

Remember, God uses anything to bring you Home, including fear and anxiety. And you are likely to be in some state of anxiety about various conditions happening both to you and to your planet at the present time. When you begin to claim your unease without pretending to be such a holy spiritual seeker that you have no fear about world events, you can really start to experience what you are feeling. You become real. You are no longer hiding from yourself. Then, and only then, can you begin to find a feeling of peace that does not depend on external events. What you are reaching for is that feeling of security that comes from knowing the power, wonder, usefulness, and creativity of just being who you are. *You, as you are, are enough.* This awareness is available to any one of you who is willing to do a minimum amount of work.

The power and energy bombarding this planet is accelerating. This power comes from the Source Itself, as Awareness Itself, and when the power is in motion, Earthly things are transformed in your sight and are revealed to be Awareness Itself. My friends, you are partly responsible for this transformation. *You* want things to be different. *You* want to be free of Earthbound illusions. *You* want to have a sense of God-Presence. Each of you, in your own way, is calling for this new life. You want transformation of the old into something totally new. And I do not mean just those in the so-called New Age movement. Every being on this planet has a soul, and within *every* soul there is a cry—and that cry is for some kind of increased awareness and understanding.

If you are at all interested in any kind of planetary or personal transformation, put your focus on what you are experiencing in your body, mind, and emotions. If it takes anxiety and fear to bring you to peace, is it not then possible to feel an inner gratitude for those things that bring you fear, and therefore awareness? Doesn't it make sense that you would have deep, abiding gratitude for all of the circumstances that brought the fear into your life in the first place? I know this is the last thing most people want to think about. It is not a popular political statement to be saying, "Be happy for your misery because it's going to bring you to awareness." But it is a very effective use of the difficult events in the world.

So what is the process that brings you to this place of peace? It begins when you *acknowledge and fully feel* any degree of fear, anxiety, or desperation in your life. Name it if you can. As spiritual seekers, you have been taught to turn away from any ugly thoughts in your mind or emotions in your body. You have also been taught to turn away from your own assessments of what is happening in your life. You have been instructed to "be the light" and "be more loving." Let me remind you that what keeps you from feeling the presence of love is fear; and you can't feel the love until you are willing to feel the fear, and sometimes even the ugliness in it. Something very interesting can happen if you will sit with these feelings and become close and intimate with them. Fear and anxiety can have many faces and move through many stages. Find out what they feel like in your body. Are they heavy? Do they constrict you? Are they hot or cold? What shape do they have? Stay with them, and you will eventually move to a place where peace can also be felt. Within that fear, within that pain, you can actually feel a peaceful space.

"But," you ask, "how do I move away from fear of a real event, such as my own death or the death of those I love? These things are really going to happen." We go back to the basics. Number one, be a friend to yourself, and face and feel the fear. That means opening up the inner door and acknowledging the entire spectrum of feelings within that fearful event. Open to it all. Let images arise; let physical sensations arise. Most of you are afraid to stay with the feelings. The first thing your mind tries to do is describe *why* you are afraid. Do not move into why, because the first little reason that pops up will be taken by your ego as sufficient to explain the feelings away. When you stay with the feelings, you create the space for something different to happen. To help yourself do this, say things like, "Fear is present now." Then, *put all of your awareness on it*. In doing so, you bring the vaster, wiser, more complete power of awareness into the presence of that smaller, more constricted energy; and they begin to blend. They begin to "influence" each other. They begin to change into something that feels very different from fear alone.

There is no way to keep fear from entering your life, and you do not need to keep all fear away. Fear is a magnificent part of the whole human experience. When you see this clearly, you will discover something very interesting. *Fear is also a kind of excitement.* Fear can make things happen, bringing interesting movement. Fear can be dynamic and life-giving. No matter how desperate you may be, there is a part of yourself that you can move through the feelings of confusion, doubt, and darkness, into clarity and understanding. That part is awake to the awareness of the magnificent substrata of consciousness—an ebullient, bubbling, radiant, peaceful feeling of life that stays with you through every experience. *Fear is often the doorway to that awakening.* Fear can be a gift if you are willing to stay in touch with it as it carries you to peace.

§ § §

There is a classic story about the death of Ramana Maharshi's mother. When Ramana cried, his disciples asked, "Why are you crying? You're enlightened!" His reply was, "It is absolutely appropriate that a son mourn the death of his mother." He shed real tears, and there was pain in his heart, but at the same moment, there was a knowing within him: "This is what it is to be human. These are the feelings and responses of a human consciousness." And he felt the beautiful sense of *appropriateness*, the *bliss* of feeling the pain of his loss. When you deeply feel loss, you may discover that you are also feeling life. The rising and falling of all kinds of experience is what it is like to be on this Earth plane. What an enlightened one knows is the incredible joy, delight, and privilege it is to be feeling them *all!*

It is a difficult concept to accept that it is a *privilege* to experience your pain, your loss, your fear, and your sorrow. So let's talk about why this is true. One reason you come into physical form is for consciousness to participate in limitation and also in the incredibly exciting expansion of Itself into new forms and new freedoms. You bring more and more awareness into all of the createdness; and as you begin to understand this purpose, you will realize that it doesn't matter so much if you are feeling happy or sorrowful about your situation. What matters is that you are feeling! You are experiencing and you are living! You discover that there is something to be found in the midst of sorrow or happiness that transcends them both and gives meaning to the sorrow or the happiness. You experience a knowing that what you are and what you do are incredibly wondrous and important, and, in the deepest sense, totally meaningful. Every breath you take, my friends, is creatively meaningful, whether you are conscious of it or not. If you learn to breathe with awareness, you will feel the power of your breath, of life itself, moving in your body every moment, in the midst of your pain, isolation, or fear. Then you will sense that each experience, in and of itself, has meaning.

You need not suffer without meaning. To suffer without meaning is death, but to suffer knowing that in the midst of it you can bring in and expand love, compassion, beauty, and humor is to experience life. When you deeply understand you came to experience life in *all* its ongoing moment-to-moment aspects, then every moment becomes as important as every other moment. You can be told that you will spend the next 20 years lying in a hospital bed, and you will still be able to bring the excitement, wonder, mystery, and wholeness of life into that incredibly limiting situation. You can take the biggest nightmare your fearful mind can create, and realize that this transformative ability can be awakened in the very midst of your horror. Then you will be able to find meaning within it—*because* you are experiencing, and experiencing is *living*—and living is *God in action.* "Your" life is God's action.

Your reason for walking this Earth is to know that every moment is essentially transmutable and transformative. As you get excited about every breath you breathe, every experience you have, every feeling you feel, realizing the importance of it all, your life takes on a totally new awareness. *Everything you do with awareness creates a moment that brings you closer to the peaceful knowing of who you are.* Breathing is beautiful. Breathe, knowing the incredible honor it is to be here in this experience, doing whatever you are doing. Realize it is breath that is the gift; it is breath that is the God; it is breath that is the Light. When you do, you will be able to say, "This moment, just as it is, is 'it,' " and know you do not need to change it, avoid it, suppress it, or make it different. When you truly understand that *each moment*, exactly as it is, is *the* moment for awareness, you will start to feel the awesome wonder of being totally in the present.

When you say you don't know how to be totally in the present, I can only tell you the same basic things I have been saying for 15 years. You stay totally present in the moment by hearing your thoughts, feeling your emotions, being aware of your body, *inside* your body. When you do, the gift of life is yours. It is the feeling that no matter how *limited* your life may be, you are still *filled* with life. This means that the paraplegic lying on a bed has the *same amount of life force* pulsating through them as anyone else, even though it is present in a way that bypasses all the neurological data available at the moment. This life force is something that is not based on your neurological system, but on an entirely different one. This life force does not depend on the senses. Rather, the senses depend totally on IT.

Science and the Mystery of Creation

In the next few years, science will be discovering more sophisticated ways of showing you who and what you are. One of these will be the "discovery" that every one of the three trillion cells in your body contains a *pulsating particle* that does not have specific form. This "particle" is going to be observed as something that is in motion and yet has a stillness to it. I am not talking here about a subatomic particle. I am talking about the substance in which all of the subatomic particles rest. Scientists will become interested in what *surrounds and upholds* the particles themselves. And as you know, when any group of disciplined beings, whether spiritually or scientifically oriented, put their awareness on seeking something, things often appear. And one of the things that will appear is a wavelike motion of "no substance" that *does not break down into anything else.*

This discovery will set off an exciting investigation as scientists become aware of all the separated atomic and subatomic particles disappearing into this other inseparable "something." They will see all these particles rise, have life, and then move back into this indivisible something. In our terminology, they will begin to pay attention to the 99 percent instead of the one percent, the "ground of Being" instead of all the various forms of being. What a mystery to unravel! What an exciting investigation will take place! What is this magnificent substance that doesn't break down, that produces forms that have life, which then drift back into it and become invisible once again? How scientists deal with this question will be a revelation for all of them.

You have the ability to find the answer yourselves in the laboratory of your own body. In each of its trillions of cells, there is something that is *now called space,* because it is nothing. That space is the basic no-thing of who you are. It contains power-packed points of pulsating "knowing." Together, these points form beautiful patterns that scientists will eventually be able to project on a screen so you can see them. They will not be physical patterns. They will be the physical manifestation of the basic pattern of your individual "invisible" energy field that you will be able to pick out from among the billions of patterns projected. In reality, you are an individual, pulsating, *magnetic* patterning of trillions of points of light and power. *All form,* no matter how different it looks from human form, has this magnificent, alive patterning. The pulsations of the pattern that make up your being are connected in infinitely varied motions with all the other particles and patterns of creation in an intricately beautiful "network." It is the *pulsation* within the pattern that keeps you alive. What is it that fuels the pulsation in the body? *The breath.* When breath ceases, the pulsation into the pattern ceases. It is not that the individual pattern then dies, fades or in any way diminishes. It simply recedes and moves out of the physical body back into the basic patterning. If I could put it this way, it drops out of the human body and merges itself with a deeper state of Being.

§ § §

When a person leaves the physical body, they sometimes find themselves in the presence of an awe-inspiring vortex that they "see" as a pulsating light. They feel an overwhelming love and compassion coming from that light. What they are experiencing is an expansion into more vast awareness. Their awareness has moved away from their physical body to a light-form they experience as being outside themselves. At this stage, there is "them" and "other." When a person has actually "died," meaning a decision has been made not to return to the Earth-body, "you" begin to be aware that what seemed to be "your" energy was always a part of the Wholeness of God's Energy. The seeming separation ends. This deeper pattern is not "out there" any longer, and you are able to merge with it because your basic pattern is made up of the same essence. You can experience this now by imagining yourself in the presence of the most loving, compassionate, accepting, magnetic field of awareness you possibly can. Allow yourself to yearn for such a possibility to appear in your awareness. As you do, also allow "yourself" to imagine what it would feel like to have there be absolutely no separation between what you see as yourself and what God Is.

In order to feel this blending, you must breathe and feel the moment with awareness. You stay in your body, steady, centered, and awake. This awareness, solidly grounded in the body, in the moment, in the "here and now," makes the blending come alive.

It is your awareness that fires off that pulsation within your cells. *Awareness* is essential, and it is always present. If all that was required was breathing, everyone would be in a state of nonseparation. If all that was required was eating pure food, then everyone eating in a health-food restaurant would be enlightened. Awareness is a conscious process. Without putting the power of your awareness on this magnificent system, you do not feel and *participate in* the firing off of those pulsating points of power and the electric life it gives. It is an awesome experience. Your smallest toe is as alive as the deepest part of your heart, and your mind is no different than your finger. All becomes an intricately joined oneness. The boundaries of separation have dissolved.

As you sit in silence, remember this blending process. "Your" field plus "God's" field can pulsate together into one pattern of power. This is why two or more people gathered together can experience tremendous explosions of consciousness. They blend together, change, and become vaster. When they go their separate ways again, their old patterns are no longer the same. A vaster, deeply vibrating new pattern is now present. Can you see how, if you have like-hearted and like-minded people whose energies are pulsating and blending together, you can feel something greater than yourself? The hope is that eventually you will know that this blending is possible every moment, endlessly. There is no end to this magnificent dance of creation.

So, we end where we began. Where do you go for your safety? What is safety? In the end, safety is knowing that *whatever* happens, God is in God's heaven and all is right with *your* world. Safety is knowing that all's well, exactly as it is, without anything being changed, added to, or taken away. And how do you get that knowing? You get it by *feeling the pulsation of that vast pattern within you.* Call it Life if you want, or call it God if you want. It is a pulsating pattern you can feel in every cell of your body. If you want to participate in that pulsation, just turn your awareness to your breath.

Be aware that it is the breath that makes the pulsation alive for you. When you are aware of both, you can sit in the midst of the biggest nightmare, feeling the nightmare, and at the same time, feeling the incredible pattern that vibrates through all of it. The pulsating pattern gives it mystery, wonder, purpose, and absolute joy. Your safety lies in feeling the endless, magnificent wisdom of that pulsating power moving through every moment of your life, telling you, "All's well. You are not alone. You could not possibly be alone. There is only the One, and You are That." There is no other safety that will withstand the pressures of this life.

Please remember one last thing: This magnetic pulsation is not lifeless. When you start to feel it moment after moment, coursing through your physical, mental, and emotional bodies, you will shed tears of gratitude. It is the most exquisite thing possible to feel in the body. All other pleasures pale beside it. You will be filled with gratitude for choosing this human assignment; and you will want to live it from that deep level of gratitude and honor for yourself and everyone else, and most of all, for the amazing wisdom that presented this possibility to you in the first place.

"I ask you to become aware of yourself as body moving, senses filled with the world, keeping nothing away, allowing everything in; the smells of life, the motion of life, the thoughts, the feeling of it all. I am asking you to become alive in your physical body in a way you are not yet accustomed to being. Every time you put your foot on the ground, you are giving something to the Earth. You either give from a place of love, compassion, humor, and understanding; or you give from a place of limitation, pain, and sorrow. Remember, there is but one world, one people, one consciousness."

— Bartholomew

About Mary-Margaret Moore

Mary-Margaret Moore spent her first 18 years growing up in Hawaii and the next 5 obtaining two degrees from Stanford University in California. She is married and has four children. She has been a seeker of clear awareness for many years, gaining clarity from the study of the Christian saints, Zen, the Sufis, Advaita, and most of all, the teachings of Ramana Maharshi.

ॐ ॐ ॐ ॐ ॐ

Books by Bartholomew

"I Come As A Brother": *A Remembrance of Illusions*

As a part of the vast, amazing Source, Bartholomew comes as a brother, teacher, and friend. Fourteen transcribed meetings deal with our relationship to ourselves, each other, and the Divine. From sexuality to St. Francis, Bartholomew's wisdom, compassion, and humor point us toward a more expanded awareness.

From the Heart of a Gentle Brother

Bartholomew brings meaningful perspective to questions about relationships, money, sexuality, drugs, and AIDS. Valuable insights are offered into the world of Devas, symbols, myths, and allies. Individual and group exercises are included to help us open to the Light that surrounds us.

Reflections of an Elder Brother: *Awakening from the Dream*

Anyone seeking to reawaken their experience of Oneness will find guidance in Bartholomew's basic message. It is his contention that we only need awaken to who we really are to find that which we seek. He reveals the illusions of self-imposed limitations and reminds us constantly that we have never been separate from the Source.

Planetary Brother

Bartholomew explores the transformative opportunities inherent in personal and global conflict. He reminds us to hold a vision of harmony, and offers steps we can take to help ourselves and our planet move toward greater peace, love, and understanding. This is the book to read for all who are longing to increase the peace in their hearts and peace on the planet.

Journeys with a Brother: *Japan to India*

A group of ordinary people find extraordinary insights with the help of Bartholomew. On a trip that takes them from the temples of Japan to the heights of the Himalayas, they travel together to experience a sacred Initiation given by the 14th Dalai Lama. It is the story of the Self accompanying Itself, delighting in all aspects of Its journey.

Ordering information may be found at the front of this book.

Notes

We hope you enjoyed this Hay House book.
If you would like to receive a free catalog featuring additional
Hay House books and products, or if you would like informa-
tion about the Hay Foundation, please contact:

Hay House, Inc.
P.O. Box 5100
Carlsbad, CA 92018-5100

(760) 431-7695 or **(800) 654-5126**
(760) 431-6948 (fax) or **(800) 650-5115 (fax)**

Please visit the Hay House Website at: **www.hayhouse.com**